# 5000 FRENCH WORDS

## Essential Vocabulary for Examinations

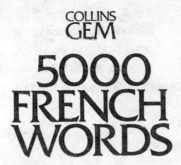

COLLINS
GEM

# 5000 FRENCH WORDS

compiled by
**Barbara I. Christie MA (Hons)**
and
**Màiri MacGinn MA (Hons)**

## Collins
### London and Glasgow

*General Editor*
**Richard H. Thomas**

First Published 1979
ISBN 0 00 459302 2

© **William Collins Sons & Co. Ltd.** 1979

Printed in Great Britain by
**Collins Clear-Type Press**

# HOW TO USE THIS BOOK

This book provides the user with a comprehensive range of vocabulary covering areas which are frequently the subject of language courses and exam questions, as well as wider interest areas which he may wish to discover for himself. There are 50 themes, each beginning with a basic list of nouns, and building up the whole subject picture through appropriate verbs, example phrases, idioms etc. The lists are equally suited to memorization, perhaps as a class exercise, and for use in essays or letters, or in conversation groups.

The nouns themselves are divided on facing pages into masculine and feminine genders. As a general rule three different levels of difficulty have been given for each theme, marked with 1, 2 and 3 stars. These serve to split the vocabulary into manageable sections for easier learning. As far as possible, each pair of facing pages is a self-contained unit. The 50 themes are further supplemented by separate vocabulary lists, grouped according to parts of speech, and containing items which are not restricted to one theme or even to a few. This brings the total number of vocabulary items to 5000.

The user will find it easy to follow ideas from one theme to another: for instance, when he is describing his house he can progress from LA MAISON—EN GÉNÉRAL to more detailed vocabulary under LA MAISON—EN PARTICULIER and LES MEUBLES. Similarly LES PARTIES DU CORPS contains vocabulary for the basic parts of the body, while diseases and other afflictions can be found in LA SANTÉ. The user will quickly become familiar with the layout of the French themes, which are arranged alphabetically, and an English version of the contents list is also provided on pages 8 and 9.

French words which have more than one meaning are marked by an asterisk (*) and a full list of such homonyms is given on page 239 with references to the various translations in different themes.

The final section in the book is a 'reminder' index allowing the user to find the French for words in the first two levels. This will serve as a valuable revision aid.

A large amount of grammatical information has been included in the text, giving all irregular plurals as well as plurals of the commonest compound words.

A colon precedes words beginning with an aspirate h (le :hibou versus l'hippopotame). Finally, words with difficult or irregular pronunciations have been given a phonetic transcription which will help, with the aid of the following chart, to settle any pronunciation problems.

| | |
|---|---|
| i as in vie, lit | ɛ̃ as in matin, plein |
| e as in blé, jouer | ɑ̃ as in sans, vent |
| ɛ as in merci, très | ɔ̃ as in bon, ombre |
| a as in patte, plat | œ̃ as in brun, lundi |
| ɑ as in bas, gras | j as in yeux, pied |
| ɔ as in mort, donner | ɥ as in lui, huile |
| o as in mot, gauche | ɲ as in agneau, vigne |
| u as in genou, roue | ŋ as in English -ing |
| y as in rue, tu | ʃ as in chat, tache |
| ø as in peu, deux | ʒ as in je, gens |
| œ as in peur, meuble | R as in rue, venir |
| ə as in le, premier | |

All other sounds are written and pronounced as in English.

BIC
MMG

# ABBREVIATIONS USED IN THIS BOOK

| | |
|---|---|
| *m* | masculine |
| *f* | feminine |
| *pl* | plural |
| *inv* | invariable, no change |
| *subj* | subjunctive |
| *n* | noun |
| *adj* | adjective |
| *adv* | adverb |
| *prep* | preposition |
| *conj* | conjunction |

**8**

## CONTENTS

## CONTENTS (cont)

9

## TABLE DES MATIÈRES     PAGE

## TABLE DES MATIÈRES (*suite*)     PAGE

* À L'AÉROPORT

| | |
|---|---|
| un **accident d'avion** | air *or* plane crash |
| un **aéroport** | airport |
| l'**air**\* | air |
| un **avion** | plane, aeroplane |
| les **bagages** | luggage |
| le **billet (ouvert)** | (open) ticket |
| le **bureau de renseignements** | information desk |
| le **départ** | departure |
| le **douanier** | customs officer |
| l'**hélicoptère** | helicopter |
| le **parachute** | parachute |
| le **passager** | passenger |
| le **passeport** | passport |
| le **pilote**\* | pilot |
| le **porteur** | porter |
| le **prix du billet** | fare |
| le **retard** | delay |
| le **touriste** | tourist |
| le **vacancier** | holiday-maker |

l'**armée** (*f*) **de l'air** the Air Force

**il est allé à Paris en avion** he went to Paris by plane *or* by air, he flew to Paris

**l'avion a pris l'air** the plane has taken off

**par avion** by airmail

**faire/défaire ses bagages** to pack/unpack (one's luggage)

**les bagages à main** hand luggage

**faire enregistrer ses bagages** to register one's luggage

**le billet aller/aller-retour** single/return ticket

**le passager clandestin** the stowaway

**le tableau des arrivées/des départs** the arrivals/departures board

**atterrir** to land, touch down

**un atterrissage forcé** a forced *or* an emergency landing

**\* À L'AÉROPORT**

| | |
|---|---|
| une **arrivée** | arrival |
| la **boîte noire** | black box |
| la **consigne** | left luggage (office) |
| la **descente** | descent |
| la **douane** | customs |
| une **entrée**\* | entrance |
| une **horloge** | (large) clock |
| la **passagère** | passenger |
| la **sortie** | exit; gate |
| la **touriste** | tourist |
| la **valise** | case, suitcase |
| la **vitesse**\* | speed |

**passer à la douane** to go through customs
**fouiller les bagages** to search the luggage
**les droits** (*mpl*) **de douane** customs duty
**exempté de douane** duty-free
**des cigarettes hors-taxe** duty-free cigarettes
**la sortie de secours**\* emergency exit
**à toute vitesse** at full *or* top speed

## ** À L'AÉROPORT

| | |
|---|---|
| un atterrissage | landing |
| un avion à réaction | jet plane |
| le décollage | take-off |
| un équipage | crew |
| un homme d'affaires | businessman |
| le steward | steward |

## *** À L'AÉROPORT

| | |
|---|---|
| un aiguilleur du ciel | air traffic controller |
| un escalier roulant | escalator |
| l'horaire, | |
| un indicateur | timetable |
| le jumbo-jet (pl jumbo-jets) | jumbo jet |
| le mal de l'air | airsickness |
| le mur du son | sound barrier |
| le radar | radar |
| le satellite | satellite terminal |
| le tapis roulant | moving pavement |
| le trou d'air | air pocket |
| le vol* | flying; flight |

un atterrissage en catastrophe a crash landing
'éteignez vos cigarettes' 'extinguish your cigarettes'
'attachez vos ceintures' 'fasten your seat belts'
avoir le mal de l'air to be airsick
passer or franchir le mur du son to break the sound barrier
il y a 8 heures de vol entre ... it's an 8-hour flight between ...
le vol numéro 776 en provenance de Madrid/à destination de Madrid flight number 776 from Madrid/to Madrid
survoler Londres to fly over London

## ** À L'AÉROPORT

| | |
|---|---|
| une aérogare | (*in town*) air terminal; (*at airport*) airport buildings |
| une aile | wing |
| une altitude | altitude |
| une ascension | climb |
| la ceinture de sécurité | seat belt |
| la correspondance | connection |
| la destination | destination |
| une étiquette | label |
| la :hauteur | height |
| l'hôtesse de l'air | air hostess |
| la piste* (d'envol) | runway |
| la salle de départ | departure lounge |

## *** À L'AÉROPORT

| | |
|---|---|
| une agence de voyages | travel agency |
| les balises de nuit | runway lights |
| les commandes | controls |
| une escale | stop-over |
| l'hélice | propeller |
| la ligne aérienne | airline |
| la réservation | reservation |
| la tour de contrôle | control tower |
| la turbulence | turbulence |

manquer sa correspondance to miss one's connection
perdre de la hauteur to lose height
prendre de la hauteur to gain height, climb
à bord (de l'avion) on board (the plane)
faire escale à New York to stop over at New York
faire une escale de 5 heures à Londres to make a 5-hour stop-over at London

**\* LES ANIMAUX**

| | |
|---|---|
| un **animal** (*pl* animaux) | animal |
| le **bœuf**\* [bœf] (*pl* -s [bø]) | ox |
| le **chat** | cat |
| le **cheval** (*pl* chevaux) | horse |
| le **chien** | dog |
| le **cochon** | pig |
| le **cou** | neck |
| un **éléphant** | elephant |
| le **lion** | lion |
| le **mouton**\* | sheep |
| le **tigre** | tiger |
| le **zoo** [zo-o] | zoo |

**\*\* LES ANIMAUX**

| | |
|---|---|
| un **âne** | donkey |
| le **chameau** (*pl* -x) | camel |
| un **écureuil** | squirrel |
| le :**hérisson** | hedgehog |
| le **kangourou** | kangaroo |
| le **lapin** | rabbit |
| le **loup** | wolf |
| un **ours** [URS] | bear |
| le **poney** | pony |
| le **renard** | fox |
| le **serpent** | snake |
| le **singe** | monkey |
| le **taureau** (*pl* -x) | bull |
| le **zèbre** | zebra |

**avoir un chat dans la gorge** to have a frog in one's throat
**à cheval** on horseback
**faire du cheval, monter à cheval** to go riding
**une promenade à cheval** a horse-ride
**un chien d'aveugle/de garde** a guide dog/guard dog
**le chien fait le beau** the dog sits up and begs
**'attention chien méchant'** 'beware of the dog'
**le lion s'est échappé du zoo** the lion escaped from the zoo

## * LES ANIMAUX, QUELQUES CARACTÉRISTIQUES

| | |
|---|---|
| la bouche | mouth (of *horse, sheep, cow*) |
| la chatte | (she-)cat |
| la chienne | (she-)dog, bitch |
| la fourrure | fur |
| la lionne | lioness |
| une oreille | ear |
| la patte | paw |
| la queue* [kø] | tail |
| la souris | mouse |
| la tigresse | tigress |
| la vache | cow |

## ** LES ANIMAUX, QUELQUES CARACTÉRISTIQUES

| | |
|---|---|
| la girafe | giraffe |
| la grenouille | frog |
| la gueule | mouth (of *dog, cat, lion, tiger*) |
| la poche* | pouch (of *kangaroo*) |
| les rayures | stripes (of *zebra*) |
| la trompe | trunk (of *elephant*) |

un animal aux longues oreilles a long-eared animal
un animal aux oreilles pointues an animal with
pointed ears
le chien dressa ses oreilles the dog pricked up its
ears
les pattes de devant/de derrière the front/hind legs
le chien a donné la patte the dog put out its paw,
the dog gave a paw
le chien a agité la queue *or* a remué la queue (ne
me voyant) the dog wagged its tail (at me)
'bas les pattes!' (*to dog*) 'down!'

*** LES ANIMAUX, QUELQUES
    CARACTÉRISTIQUES

| | |
|---|---|
| les bois | antlers |
| le bouc | (billy) goat |
| le cerf [SER] | deer, stag |
| le cobaye | guinea-pig |
| le crapaud | toad |
| le crocodile | crocodile |
| le :hamster | hamster |
| l'hippopotame | hippopotamus |
| le lièvre | hare |
| le mulet | mule |
| le museau (pl -x) | snout (of pig) |
| un ours blanc | polar bear |
| le phoque | seal |
| le piège | trap |
| les piquants | spines (of hedgehog) |
| le poil | coat, hair |
| le porc* | pig |
| le rhinocéros | rhinoceros |
| le sabot | hoof |

**aller à dos d'âne/de chameau** to ride on a donkey/a
  camel
**aller à la chasse au renard** to go fox-hunting
**une course de taureaux** a bullfight
**les courses** (fpl) **de taureaux** bullfighting
**libérer un animal** to set an animal free
**nous avons 12 animaux/nous n'avons pas d'animaux
  chez nous** we have 12 pets/no pets (in our house)

### \*\*\* LES ANIMAUX, QUELQUES CARACTÉRISTIQUES

| | |
|---|---|
| la baleine | whale |
| la bosse | hump (*of camel*) |
| la caractéristique | characteristic |
| la carapace | shell (*of tortoise*) |
| la chauve-souris | bat |
| la chèvre | (nanny-)goat |
| la corne | horn |
| la couleuvre | grass snake |
| la crinière | mane (*of lion, horse*) |
| les défenses | tusks |
| la griffe | claw |
| la jument | mare |
| la mule | mule |
| la ramure | antlers |
| la taupe | mole |
| la tortue | tortoise |

le chat sortit *or* montra ses griffes the cat showed its claws

le chat rentra ses griffes the cat drew in its claws

## LES ANIMAUX—OÙ HABITENT-ILS?

| | |
|---|---|
| **une abeille** (bee) | **la ruche** (beehive) |
| **un aigle** (eagle) | **une aire** (eyrie) |
| **le cheval** (horse) | **une écurie** (stable) |
| **le chien** (dog) | **la niche** (kennel) |
| **le lapin** (rabbit) | **le terrier** (burrow) |
| | **la garenne** (warren) |
| | **la cage à lapins** (hutch) |
| **le lion, un ours, le tigre** (lion, bear, tiger) | **la tanière, un antre** (den, lair) |
| **le mouton** (sheep) | **le parc à moutons** (sheep-pen) |
| **un oiseau** (bird) | **le nid** (nest) |
| **la perruche** (budgie) | **la cage** (cage) |
| **le poisson rouge** (goldfish) | **le bocal à poissons** (goldfish bowl) |
| **le porc, le cochon** (pig) | **la porcherie** (pigsty) |
| **la poule** (hen) | **le poulailler** (henhouse) |
| **la vache** (cow) | **une étable** (cowshed, byre) |

## LES ANIMAUX, LEURS PETITS ET LES BRUITS QU'ILS FONT

| | | |
|---|---|---|
| un âne | le petit âne | braire (*to bray*) hi-han! (*heehaw!*) |
| le bétail la vache | le veau | beugler, meugler, mugir (*to bellow:* *bull*) (*to moo: cow*) meuh! (*moo!*) |
| le canard | le caneton, le canardeau | faire coin-coin (*to quack*) coin-coin! (*quack, quack!*) |
| le chat | le chaton, le petit chat | ronronner (*to purr*) miauler (*to miaow*) miaou! (*miaow!*) |
| le cheval | le poulain | hennir (*to neigh*) |
| la chèvre | le chevreau | bêler, chevroter (*to bleat*) |
| le chien | le chiot | aboyer (*to bark*) grogner (*to growl*) oua, oua! (*bow-wow!*) |
| le cochon, | le porcelet, le petit cochon | grogner (*to grunt*) |
| le lion | le lionceau | rugir (*to roar*) |
| le mouton | un agneau | bêler (*to bleat*) bê! (*baa!*) |
| une oie | un oison | siffler (*to hiss*) cacarder (*to honk*) coin-coin! (*oink, oink!*) |
| la poule | le poussin | chanter (*to crow: cock*) glousser (*to cluck*) piauler (*to cheep*) cocorico! (*cock-a-doodle-do!*) |
| le renard | le renardeau | aboyer (*to bark*) |

## * LES ARBRES

| | |
|---|---|
| un arbre | tree |
| un arbre de Noël | Christmas tree |
| le bois | wood |
| le tronc | trunk |

## ** LES ARBRES

| | |
|---|---|
| un arbre fruitier | fruit tree |
| le feuillage | leaves, foliage |
| le rameau (pl -x) | branch |
| le tilleul | lime tree |
| le verger | orchard |

## *** LES ARBRES

| | |
|---|---|
| le bouleau (pl -x) | birch |
| le bourgeon | bud |
| le buis | box tree |
| le buisson | bush |
| le châtaignier | chestnut tree |
| le chêne | oak |
| un érable | maple |
| le frêne | ash |
| le :hêtre | beech |
| le :hêtre rouge | copper beech |
| le :houx | holly |
| un if | yew |
| le marronnier | (horse) chestnut tree |
| un orme | elm |
| le peuplier | poplar |
| le pin | pine |
| le platane | plane tree |
| le sapin | fir tree |
| le saule (pleureur) | (weeping) willow |
| le vignoble | vineyard |

**grimper sur un arbre** to climb a tree
**couper** or **abattre un arbre** to fell a tree
**l'arbre généalogique** the family tree
**une chaise de** or **en bois** a wooden chair
**les décorations de Noël** Christmas decorations

**\* LES ARBRES**

| | |
|---|---|
| la branche | branch |
| la feuille | leaf |
| la forêt | forest |

**\*\* LES ARBRES**

| | |
|---|---|
| l'écorce | bark |
| la racine | root |

**\*\*\* LES ARBRES**

| | |
|---|---|
| une aubépine | hawthorn |
| la baie* | berry |

les feuilles de thé tea leaves
une cabane construite dans un arbre a tree house
la cime d'un arbre a treetop
une pomme de pin a pine cone, a fir cone

**\* L'AUTO ET LA ROUTE**

| | |
|---|---|
| un **accident** (de la route) | road accident |
| un **agent** de police | policeman |
| un **automobiliste** | motorist |
| le **camion** | lorry, truck |
| le **camionneur** | lorry driver |
| le **chauffeur**\* | driver; chauffeur |
| le **code** de la route | the Highway code |
| le **conducteur** | driver |
| le **cycliste** | cyclist |
| le **détour** | detour |
| les **feux** (de circulation) | traffic lights |
| le **frein** | brake |
| le **garage** | garage |
| le **kilomètre** | kilometer |
| le **klaxon** | horn, hooter |
| le **moteur** | engine |
| le **pare-brise** (pl inv) | windscreen |
| le **parking** | car park |
| le **permis** de conduire | driving licence |
| le **phare**\* | headlight; headlamp |
| le **piéton** | pedestrian |
| le **pneu** | tyre |

**brûler un feu rouge** to go through a red light

**le feu arrière** the rear light

**200 kilomètres à l'heure** 200 kilometres an hour

**mettre le moteur en marche** to start (up) *or* switch on the engine; **couper le moteur** to switch off the engine

**dans un grincement de freins** with a screech of brakes; **freiner brusquement** to brake sharply

**klaxonner, donner un coup de klaxon** to sound *or* toot one's horn

**le pare-brise a volé en éclats** the windscreen shattered

**crever, avoir un pneu crevé** to have a puncture; **être à plat** to have a flat tyre

**l'examen du permis de conduire** the driving test

**garer (la voiture)** to park (the car)

**\* L'AUTO ET LA ROUTE**

| | |
|---|---|
| une auto, une automobile | car |
| une autoroute (à péage) | (toll) motorway |
| la caravane | caravan |
| la carte routière | road map |
| la circulation | traffic |
| la crevaison | puncture |
| l'essence | petrol |
| l'huile | oil |
| la panne | breakdown |
| la portière | (car) door |
| la roue | wheel |
| la route | road |
| la station-service | service station, filling station |
| la vitesse* | speed; gear |
| la voiture* | car |

conduire une voiture to drive a car
faire une promenade en voiture to go for a drive
faites le plein (d'essence)! fill her up please!
la roue avant/arrière the front/rear wheel
la roue de secours the spare wheel
la route nationale trunk or main road
prenez la route de Lyon take the road to Lyons
perdre/retrouver sa route to lose/find one's way
la route sera longue it'll be a long journey
il y a 3 heures de route it's a 3-hour journey
se mettre en route to start out, set off
en route (adv) en route, on the way
en route! let's go!, let's be off!
bonne route! have a good journey!
changer de vitesse to change gear
être or tomber en panne to break down, have a breakdown
je suis tombé en panne sèche I've run out of petrol
doubler or dépasser une voiture to overtake a car
faire entretenir/faire réparer sa voiture to have one's car serviced/repaired

## ** L'AUTO ET LA ROUTE

| | |
|---|---|
| l'auto-stop | hitch-hiking |
| un auto-stoppeur | hitch-hiker |
| le blessé | casualty |
| le capot | bonnet |
| le carrefour | crossroads |
| le chauffard | road-hog |
| le coffre* | boot |
| le compteur de vitesse | speedometer |
| le conducteur débutant | learner driver |
| le démarreur | starter |
| un excès de vitesse | speeding |
| le garagiste | garage owner, garage man |
| un itinéraire | itinerary, journey |
| le mécanicien* | mechanic |
| le mort | dead man |
| le motocycliste | motorcyclist |
| le panneau (pl -x) | road sign |
| le parcmètre | parking meter |
| le pare-boue (pl inv) | mud flap |
| le pare-chocs (pl inv) | bumper |
| le poste d'essence | filling station |
| le procès-verbal, le P.-V. | fine, (parking) ticket |
| le routier | long-distance lorry driver |
| le signal routier | road sign |
| le starter | choke |
| le volant | steering wheel |

faire de l'auto-stop to go hitch-hiking

une contravention pour excès de vitesse a fine for speeding

nous roulions à toute vitesse we were driving (along) at full speed or at top speed

ralentir to slow down; s'arrêter to stop

accélérer to accelerate

le moteur démarre the engine starts up

la voiture démarre the car moves off

## ** L'AUTO ET LA ROUTE

| | |
|---|---|
| une agglomération | built-up area |
| une auto-école (*pl* auto-écoles) | driving school |
| une auto-stoppeuse (*pl* auto-stoppeuses) | hitch-hiker |
| la capote | hood |
| la ceinture de sécurité | seat belt |
| la consommation d'essence | petrol consumption |
| la contravention | traffic offence |
| la dépanneuse | breakdown van |
| la déviation | diversion |
| les heures d'affluence | rush hour, the peak period |
| la leçon de conduite | driving lesson |
| la marque | make (*of car*) |
| la mort | death |
| la morte | dead woman |
| la pédale | pedal |

**mettre une contravention** *or* **une P.-V. à quelqu'un**
to give somebody a parking ticket; to book somebody

**aux heures d'affluence** at the rush hour, at the peak period

**mettre** *or* **attacher sa ceinture de sécurité** to put on
*or* fasten one's seat belt

**'serrez à droite'** 'keep to the right'

**le moniteur d'auto-école** the driving instructor

## \*\*\* L'AUTO ET LA ROUTE

| | |
|---|---|
| un **accélérateur** | accelerator |
| un **accotement stabilisé** | hard shoulder |
| un **arrêt d'urgence** | emergency stop |
| le **bas-côté** | verge |
| le **carburateur** | carburettor |
| le **clignotant** | indicator |
| le **contractuel** | traffic warden |
| le **cric** | jack |
| le **dégagement** | clearance, headroom |
| un **enjoliveur** | hubcap |
| un **essuie-glace** (*pl inv*) | windscreen wiper |
| le **lave-auto** | car-wash |
| le **motard** | motorcycle cop |
| le **périphérique** | ring road |
| le **point mort** | neutral (gear) |
| le **pompiste** | petrol pump attendant |
| le **rétroviseur** | rear-view mirror, driving mirror |
| le **rond-point** (*pl ronds-points*) | roundabout |
| le **tournant**, le **virage** | turning, bend |

**appuyer sur le champignon** to step on the gas
**'accès interdit'** 'no entry'
**'priorité à droite'** 'give way to the right'
**'stationnement interdit'** 'no parking'
**'travaux'** 'road works'

**\*\*\* L'AUTO ET LA ROUTE**

| | |
|---|---|
| l'accélération | acceleration |
| une aire de services | service area |
| une aire de stationnement | lay-by |
| la bagnole | (old) car, banger |
| la bande médiane | central reservation |
| la boîte de vitesses | gearbox |
| une bretelle d'accès, | |
| une bretelle de raccordement | access road (to motorway) |
| la caisse* | body, bodywork |
| la conduite intérieure | saloon car |
| la contractuelle | traffic warden |
| la file (de voitures) | line (of cars), lane |
| la galerie | roof rack |
| la limitation de vitesse | speed limit, speed restriction |
| la pédale d'embrayage | clutch (pedal) |
| la plaque d'immatriculation, | |
| la plaque minéralogique | number plate |
| la remorque | trailer |
| la voie* | way, road; lane (on road) |
| la voie de raccordement | slip road |

la voiture de location rented *or* hired car
la voiture de sport sports car
la voiture avec conduite à droite right-hand drive car
déraper to skid
la voiture s'est écrasée contre le mur the car crashed into the wall
heurter une voiture to bump into a car

**\* LA BICYCLETTE**

| | |
|---|---|
| le cyclisme | cycling |
| le cycliste | cyclist |
| le frein | brake |
| le pneu | tyre |
| le vélo | bike |

**\*\* LA BICYCLETTE**

| | |
|---|---|
| le garde-boue *(pl inv)* | mudguard |
| le guidon | handlebars |
| le pare-boue *(pl inv)* | mud flap |
| le timbre\* | bell |
| le porte-bagages *(pl inv)* | luggage rack |

**\*\*\* LA BICYCLETTE**

| | |
|---|---|
| le catadioptre, le cataphote | reflector |
| le moyeu *(pl -x)* | hub |
| le rayon\* | spoke |
| le réflecteur | reflector |

**faire du cyclisme** to go in for cycling
**les freins ont lâché** the brakes failed
**freiner brusquement** to brake suddenly
**crever, avoir un pneu crevé** to have a puncture
**être à plat** to have a flat tyre
**réparer un pneu crevé** to mend a puncture
**faire marcher la sonnette** to ring the bell
**gonfler les pneus** to blow up the tyres
**il est venu en vélo** he came on his bike

## * LA BICYCLETTE

| | |
|---|---|
| la bicyclette | bicycle |
| la chaîne* | chain |
| la crevaison | puncture |
| la lampe | lamp |
| la pompe | pump |
| la roue | wheel |
| la vitesse* | speed; gear |

## ** LA BICYCLETTE

| | |
|---|---|
| la barre | crossbar |
| la dynamo | dynamo |
| la pédale | pedal |
| la pente | slope |
| la sacoche* (de bicyclette) | saddlebag, pannier |
| la selle | saddle, seat |
| la sonnette | bell |

## *** LA BICYCLETTE

| | |
|---|---|
| la côte* | slope, hill (*on road*) |
| la trousse de secours pour crevaisons | puncture repair kit |
| la valve | valve |

monter à bicyclette to get onto one's bike
aller à bicyclette to ride a bicycle
aller à la ville à *or* en bicyclette to go to town by bicycle, to cycle to town
faire une promenade à *or* en bicyclette to go for a bike ride
la roue avant/arrière the front/back wheel
changer de vitesse to change gear
à toute vitesse at full *or* top speed
monter/descendre la côte to go uphill/downhill
rouillé rusty
brillant, reluisant shiny

**\* LES BIJOUX ET LE MAQUILLAGE**

| | |
|---|---|
| l'argent* | silver |
| le bijou (pl -x) | jewel |
| le diamant | diamond |
| le miroir | mirror |
| l'or | gold |

**\*\* LES BIJOUX ET LE MAQUILLAGE**

| | |
|---|---|
| le bracelet | bracelet, bangle |
| le collier | necklace, beads |
| le kleenex | (paper) tissue |
| le maquillage | make-up |
| le parfum | perfume, scent |
| le porte-clefs (pl inv) | key-ring |
| le salon de beauté | beauty salon or parlour |
| le trésor | treasure |

**\*\*\* LES BIJOUX ET LE MAQUILLAGE**

| | |
|---|---|
| le bigoudi | curler, roller |
| le bouton de manchette | cufflink |
| le collier (de chien) | choker |
| le diadème | tiara |
| le dissolvant | nail varnish remover |
| le fard | make-up |
| le fard à paupières | eye-shadow |
| le fond de teint | foundation |
| l'orbe | orb |
| le pendentif | pendant |
| le poudrier | (powder) compact |
| le rimmel | mascara |
| le rouge à lèvres | lipstick |
| le rubis | ruby |
| le saphir | sapphire |
| le sceptre | sceptre |
| le vernis à ongles | nail varnish, nail polish |

**se farder, se maquiller** to make oneself up
**se coiffer** to do one's hair; **se brosser les cheveux**
to brush one's hair; **se peigner** to comb one's hair

---

**\* LES BIJOUX ET LE MAQUILLAGE**

| | |
|---|---|
| la bague | ring |
| la beauté | beauty |
| la chaîne\*, | |
| la chaînette | chain |
| la montre | watch |
| la perle | pearl |

**\*\* LES BIJOUX ET LE MAQUILLAGE**

| | |
|---|---|
| la coiffure | hairstyle |
| la couronne | crown |

**\*\*\* LES BIJOUX ET LE MAQUILLAGE**

| | |
|---|---|
| une alliance | wedding ring |
| la boucle d'oreille | |
| (pl boucles | |
| d'oreilles) | earring |
| la broche | brooch |
| la ceinture | belt |
| la crème de beauté | face cream |
| l'eau de toilette | toilet water |
| une émeraude | emerald |
| une épingle de cravate | tie-pin |
| la glace\* | mirror |
| la gourmette | identity bracelet |
| la manucure | manicure |
| la perruque | wig |
| la poudre (de riz) | face powder |

regarder sa montre to look at one's watch
précieux precious; de valeur valuable; sans valeur
 worthless
faire sa toilette to have a wash, get washed
être à sa toilette to be dressing, be getting ready
se raser to shave
se démaquiller to take off or remove one's make-up
se vernir les ongles to varnish one's nails

## * AU BORD DE LA MER

| | |
|---|---|
| le baigneur | bather, swimmer |
| le bain* (de mer) | bathe (*in sea*), swim |
| au bord de la mer | at the seaside; to the seaside |
| le château (*pl* -x) de sable | sandcastle |
| le courant | current |
| le maillot* (de bain) | swimming *or* bathing trunks *or* costume, swimsuit |
| le marin, le matelot | sailor |
| le passager | passenger |
| le phare* | lighthouse |
| le pique-nique (*pl* pique-niques) | picnic |
| le port* | port, harbour |
| le prix du billet | fare |
| le sable | sand |
| le slip de bain | swimming *or* bathing trunks; bikini pants |
| le vacancier | holiday-maker |

## ** AU BORD DE LA MER

| | |
|---|---|
| un aviron | oar |
| le bateau (*pl* -x) de pêche | fishing boat |
| le bikini | bikini |
| le coquillage | shell |
| un équipage | crew |
| le fond | bottom |
| à l'horizon | on the horizon |
| un océan | ocean |
| le pêcheur | fisherman |
| le pédalo | pedal-boat |
| le pont* | deck (*of ship*) |
| le rocher | rock |
| le télescope | telescope |

aller se baigner to go for a swim

pique-niquer, faire un pique-nique to go for a picnic, have a picnic

le panier à pique-nique the picnic basket, the picnic hamper

**\* AU BORD DE LA MER**

| | |
|---|---|
| une ancre | anchor |
| la côte\* | coast |
| l'eau | water |
| une île | island |
| la marée basse/haute | low/high tide |
| la mer | sea |
| la natation | swimming |
| la passagère | passenger |
| la pierre | stone, rock |
| à la plage | on the beach; to the beach |
| la promenade\* | trip, outing; walk |
| la vague | wave |

**\*\* AU BORD DE LA MER**

| | |
|---|---|
| la baie\* | bay |
| la ceinture de sauvetage | lifebelt |
| la falaise | cliff |
| les lunettes de soleil | sunglasses |
| la marine | navy |
| la rame | oar |
| la traversée | crossing |
| la voile | sail |

lever l'ancre to weigh anchor
en haute mer, en pleine mer out at sea, on the open sea
au fond de la mer at the bottom of the sea
une promenade à dos d'âne a donkey-ride
faire une promenade en bateau to go for a boat trip
'promenade' 'sea front'
flotter to float (*object*); faire la planche to float (on one's back)
la planche de surf the surfboard
faire de la voile to sail, go sailing

***AU BORD DE LA MER

| | |
|---|---|
| l'air marin | sea air |
| le bac* | ferry(-boat) |
| le caillou (pl -x) | pebble |
| le cap [kap] | point |
| le coup de soleil | sunstroke |
| les flots | waves |
| le gouvernail | rudder |
| le maître nageur | lifeguard |
| le mal de mer | seasickness |
| le mât | mast |
| le matelas pneumatique | air-bed, li-lo |
| le naufrage | shipwreck |
| les naufragés | people who are shipwrecked |
| le pavillon* | flag |
| le port de plaisance | marina |
| le quai* [ke] | quay, quayside |
| le radeau (pl -x) | raft |
| le rivage | coast, shore |
| le seau (pl -x) | bucket |
| le vaisseau (pl -x) | vessel |
| le vapeur | steamer |

couler to sink; plonger to dive
aller faire trempette to go for a paddle
éclabousser to splash
chavirer to capsize
trempé or mouillé jusqu'aux os soaked to the skin,
   wet through
se noyer to drown, be drowned
faire du surf, surfer to go surfing
le bateau a mis le cap sur Cannes the boat headed
   for Cannes
avoir le mal de mer to be seasick
aller à la dérive, être emporté par le vent to drift

*** AU BORD DE LA MER

| | |
|---|---|
| les algues | seaweed |
| la barque | small boat |
| la bouée | buoy |
| la cargaison | cargo |
| la cheminée* | funnel |
| la crème solaire | sun(-tan) cream |
| la croisière | cruise |
| l'écume | foam |
| une embouchure | mouth (of river) |
| une épave | wreck |
| la flotte | fleet |
| une insolation | (touch of) sunstroke |
| la jetée | pier; jetty |
| les jumelles* | binoculars |
| la mouette | seagull |
| la passerelle | gangway; bridge (of ship) |
| la pelle* | spade |

**partir en croisière, faire une croisière** to go on a cruise
**on en ramasse à la pelle** there are loads of them
**se faire bronzer** to get tanned
**être bronzé** to be tanned
**peler** to peel

## LES SAISONS (fpl)

| | |
|---|---|
| le printemps | spring |
| l'été (m) | summer |
| l'automne (m) | autumn |
| l'hiver (m) | winter |

**au printemps** in spring
**en été/automne/hiver** in summer/autumn/winter

## LES MOIS (mpl)

| | | | |
|---|---|---|---|
| **janvier** | January | **juillet** | July |
| **février** | February | **août** | August |
| **mars** | March | **septembre** | September |
| **avril** | April | **octobre** | October |
| **mai** | May | **novembre** | November |
| **juin** | June | **décembre** | December |

**en mai** etc, **au mois de mai** etc in May etc
**le premier avril** April Fools' Day
**le premier mai** May Day
**le cinq novembre** (anniversaire de la Conspiration des Poudres) Guy Fawkes Night
**le quatorze juillet** Bastille Day (French national holiday)
**le quinze août** Assumption (French national holiday)

## LES JOURS (mpl) DE LA SEMAINE

| | |
|---|---|
| **lundi** | Monday |
| **mardi** | Tuesday |
| **mercredi** | Wednesday |
| **jeudi** | Thursday |
| **vendredi** | Friday |
| **samedi** | Saturday |
| **dimanche** | Sunday |

**le samedi** etc on Saturdays etc
**samedi** etc on Saturday etc
**samedi** etc **prochain/dernier** next/last Saturday etc
**le samedi** etc **précédent/suivant** the previous/following Saturday etc

le dimanche des **Rameaux**/de **Pâques** Palm/Easter Sunday
le **lundi** de **Pâques**/de **Pentecôte** Easter/Whit Monday
**Mardi gras** Shrove *or* Pancake Tuesday
**mercredi des Cendres** Ash Wednesday
le **jeudi** de l'**Ascension** Ascension Day
le **jeudi saint** Maundy Thursday
le **vendredi saint** Good Friday

| | |
|---|---|
| le jour de l'An | New Year's Day |
| le réveillon du jour de l'an | New Year's Eve dinner *or* party |
| le jour J | D-Day |
| le jour des Morts | All Souls' Day |
| le jour des Rois | Epiphany, Twelfth Night |
| | |
| l'Avent (*m*) | Advent |
| le Carême | Lent |
| la Marseillaise | the Marseillaise (*French national anthem*) |
| | |
| Noël (*m*) | Christmas |
| à (la) Noël | at Christmas |
| le jour de Noël | Christmas Day |
| la veille de Noël, la nuit de Noël | Christmas Eve |
| le lendemain de Noël | Boxing Day |
| l'Pâques (*fpl*) | Easter |
| le jour de Pâques | Easter Day |
| Pâque (*f*) juive | Passover |
| le poisson d'avril | April fool; April fool's trick |
| | |
| la Saint-Sylvestre | New Year's Eve, Hogmanay |
| la Saint-Valentin | St. Valentine's Day |
| la Toussaint | All Saints' Day |
| la veille de la Toussaint | Hallowe'en |
| le drapeau tricolore | the (French) tricolour |
| prendre de bonnes résolutions | to make good resolutions |

## LES ÉVÉNEMENTS SPÉCIAUX

| | |
|---|---|
| un anniversaire | birthday |
| un anniversaire de mariage | wedding anniversary |
| le bal | dance |
| le baptême | christening, baptism |
| le cadeau (*pl* -x) | present |
| le char fleuri | decorated float |
| le cimetière | churchyard, cemetery |
| le cirque | circus |
| les confettis (*mpl*) | confetti |
| le cortège | procession |
| le décès | death |
| le défilé | procession; march |
| le divorce | divorce |
| le drapeau (*pl* -x) | flag |
| un enterrement | funeral, burial |
| le faire-part (de mariage) (*pl inv*) | wedding announcement; wedding invitation |
| le festival | festival |
| le feu d'artifice* | firework; firework display |
| le feu de joie | bonfire |
| le mariage | marriage |
| le témoin du marié | best man |

**célébrer** *or* **fêter son anniversaire** to celebrate one's birthday
**le bal du Nouvel An** New Year's Eve dance
**offrir un cadeau à quelqu'un** to give somebody a present
**tirer des feux d'artifice** to set off fireworks
**le jour de leur mariage** (on) their wedding day
**se fiancer (à** *or* **avec)** to get engaged (to)
**épouser quelqu'un, se marier avec quelqu'un** to marry somebody, get married to somebody
**divorcer** to get divorced (*of couple*)
**enterrer, ensevelir** to bury
**en deuil** in mourning

## LES ÉVÉNEMENTS SPÉCIAUX

| | |
|---|---|
| la cérémonie | ceremony |
| la demoiselle d'honneur | bridesmaid |
| les étrennes | New Year's gift; Christmas box |
| la fanfare* | brass band |
| la fête* | saint's day; fête, fair |
| la fête folklorique | festival of folk music |
| la fête foraine | (fun) fair |
| les fiançailles | engagement |
| la foire | (fun) fair |
| la lune de miel | honeymoon |
| la majorette | majorette |
| la mort | death |
| la naissance | birth |
| les noces | wedding |
| la retraite | retirement |

**aller à la noce de quelqu'un** to go to somebody's wedding

**les noces d'argent/d'or/de diamant** silver/golden/diamond wedding

**prendre sa retraite** to retire, go into retirement

**fleurir la ville** to decorate the town with flowers

**toute la ville a pavoisé** there were flags out all over town

**soyez le** *or* **la bienvenu(e)** (*pl* **les bienvenu(e)s**) you are very welcome

**féliciter quelqu'un de** *or* **sur quelque chose** to congratulate somebody on something

**souhaiter la bonne année à quelqu'un** to wish somebody a happy New Year

**souhaiter bonne chance à quelqu'un** to wish somebody (the best of) luck

**\* À LA CAMPAGNE**

| | |
|---|---|
| l'air\* | air |
| un arbre | tree |
| le bois | wood |
| le bruit | noise |
| le champ | field |
| le chasseur\* | hunter |
| le château (*pl* -x) | castle |
| le chemin (de) | path, way (to) |
| le fermier | farmer |
| le gendarme | gendarme |
| l'habitant | inhabitant |
| le lac | lake |
| le moulin (à vent) | (wind)mill |
| le pays\* | country; district |
| le pont\* | bridge |
| le ruisseau (*pl* -x) | stream |
| le sentier | path |
| le terrain\* | soil; ground |
| le touriste | tourist |
| le trou | hole |
| le village | village |

**en plein air** in the open air
**sortir prendre l'air** to go out for some fresh air
**un château hanté** a haunted castle
**ils ont fait tout le chemin à pied/en bicyclette**
  they walked/cycled the whole way
**au retour, sur le chemin du retour** on the way back
**les gens du pays** the local people, the locals
**habiter la campagne/la ville** to live in the country/
  the town
**traverser un pont** to cross a bridge
**la rivière/le ruisseau coule** the river/the stream
  flows

## * À LA CAMPAGNE

| | |
|---|---|
| la barrière* | gate |
| la botte (de caoutchouc) | (wellington) boot |
| la boue | mud |
| la camionnette | (small) van |
| à la campagne | in the country; to the country |
| la canne* | cane, (walking) stick |
| la caverne | cave |
| la chaussée | roadway |
| la colline | hill |
| la ferme | farm, farmhouse |
| la feuille | leaf |
| la forêt | forest |
| la :haie | hedge |
| la montagne | mountain |
| la paix | peace |
| la pente | slope |
| la pierre | stone, rock |
| la rivière | river |
| la route | road |
| la terre | earth, ground |
| la tour | tower |
| la touriste | tourist |
| la tranquillité | peace |

cultiver la terre to cultivate or till the land
traverser une forêt to go through a forest
se diriger vers to make one's way towards

## ** À LA CAMPAGNE

| | |
|---|---|
| un agriculteur | farmer |
| le bâton | stick |
| les campagnards | countryfolk, country people |
| le curé | vicar, priest |
| un étang | pond |
| le fleuve | river |
| le foin | hay |
| le fossé | ditch |
| le :hameau (pl -x) | hamlet |
| le paysage | countryside, landscape, scenery |
| le paysan | country man, farmer |
| le sommet | top (of hill) |

## *** À LA CAMPAGNE

| | |
|---|---|
| le blé | corn; wheat |
| le bouton-d'or (pl boutons-d'or) | buttercup |
| le buisson | bush |
| le caillou (pl -x) | pebble |
| le cottage | cottage |
| le garde champêtre | rural policeman |
| le jonc [ʒɔ̃] | reed |
| le marais | marsh |
| le piège | trap |
| le poteau (pl -x) indicateur | signpost |
| le poteau (pl -x) télégraphique | telegraph pole |
| le pré | meadow |
| le pylône | pylon |

**arriver au sommet d'une colline** to reach the top of a hill
**tomber dans un piège** to fall into a trap
**paisible** peaceful
**s'égarer** to get lost, lose one's way

## ** À LA CAMPAGNE

| | |
|---|---|
| l'agriculture | agriculture |
| une auberge | inn |
| une auberge de jeunesse | youth hostel |
| la chasse | hunting; shooting |
| la chute d'eau | waterfall |
| les jumelles* | binoculars |
| la moisson | harvest |
| la paysanne | country woman, peasant |
| la plaine | plain |
| la poussière | dust |
| la propriété | property, estate |
| la récolte | crop, harvest |
| la rive | bank (of river) |
| la vallée | valley |
| la vendange | grape harvest |

## *** À LA CAMPAGNE

| | |
|---|---|
| la bruyère | heather |
| la carrière* | quarry |
| la chaumière | (thatched) cottage |
| la commune | village, community |
| la côte* | slope, hill (on road) |
| une écluse | lock (on canal) |
| la grotte | cave |
| la lande | moor, heath |
| la mare | pond |
| les ruines | ruins |
| la source | spring, source |

aller passer ses vacances en auberges de jeunesse to go youth-hostelling

aller à la chasse au renard to go fox-hunting

grimper une colline to climb (up) a hill

à l'époque de la moisson at harvest time

faire la moisson, moissonner to harvest, reap

faire la récolte, rentrer la moisson to bring in the harvest, bring in the crops

faire les vendanges to harvest the grapes

## * LE CHEMIN DE FER

| | |
|---|---|
| les bagages | luggage |
| le billet | ticket |
| le chef de gare | stationmaster |
| le chef de train | guard |
| le chemin de fer | railway |
| le compartiment | compartment |
| le conducteur | (train-)driver |
| le contrôleur | ticket collector |
| le départ | departure |
| le filet* | luggage rack |
| le frein | brake |
| le guichet* | booking office |
| l'horaire, un indicateur | timetable |
| le métro | underground (railway) |
| le numéro | number |
| le passage à niveau | level crossing |
| le passeport | passport |
| le pont* | bridge |
| le porteur | porter |
| le prix du ticket or du billet | fare |
| le quai* [ke] | platform |
| le train | train |
| le trajet, le voyage | journey |
| le voyageur | traveller |
| le wagon | carriage, coach |

faire/défaire ses bagages to pack/unpack (one's luggage)
poinçonner, composter to punch
le billet simple the single ticket
le (billet) aller et retour the return ticket
voyager en train to travel by train or by rail
envoyer par (le) train or par chemin de fer to send by rail
freiner brusquement to brake sharply
monter dans le train to get (up) into the train
descendre du train to get (down) out of the train
manquer le train to miss the train; prendre le train to take or catch the train

* LE CHEMIN DE FER

| une arrivée | arrival |
| la barrière* | barrier |
| la bicyclette | bicycle |
| la classe | class |
| la consigne | left luggage office |
| la destination | destination |
| la direction | direction |
| une entrée* | entrance |
| la gare | station |
| l'horloge | (large) clock |
| la place* | seat |
| la portière | (carriage) door |
| la salle d'attente | waiting room |
| la sortie | exit |
| la valise | case, suitcase |
| la voie* | platform |
| la voie* (ferrée) | (railway) line or track |
| la voiture* | carriage, coach |

le train entre en gare the train enters the station

le train sort de la gare, le train quitte la gare the
train leaves the station

le train est en gare the train is in the station

le compartiment de première (classe)/de deuxième
(classe) first-class/second-class compartment

c'est pris?/libre? is this seat taken?/free?

un compartiment fumeur/non-fumeur a smoking/
non-smoking compartment

cette place est prise this seat is taken

en voiture! all aboard!

le train numéro 617 en provenance de Paris/à
destination de Paris train number 617 from Paris/
to Paris

## ** LE CHEMIN DE FER

| | |
|---|---|
| le **buffet**\* | station buffet |
| le **coup de sifflet** | blast on whistle |
| un **express** | fast train |
| le **mécanicien**\* | engine-driver |
| un **omnibus** | slow train |
| les **rails** | rails |
| le **rapide** | express train |
| le **retard** | delay |
| le **signal d'alarme** | alarm, communication cord |
| le **train express** | fast train |
| le **train de marchandises** | goods train |
| le **train omnibus** | slow train |
| le **train rapide** | express train |
| le **wagon-lit** | sleeping car |
| le **wagon-restaurant** | dining car |

## *** LE CHEMIN DE FER

| | |
|---|---|
| le **chauffeur**\* | fireman, stoker |
| le **cheminot** | railwayman |
| le **déraillement** | derailment |
| un **escalier roulant** | escalator |
| le **fourgon du chef de train** | guard's van |
| le **supplément** | extra charge |

**aller chercher quelqu'un à la gare** to go and fetch somebody from the station

**accompagner quelqu'un à la gare** to go with somebody to the station

**descendre les bagages du filet** to take down the luggage from the rack

**'ne pas se pencher au dehors'** 'do not lean out of the window'

**dérailler** to become derailed

** LE CHEMIN DE FER

| | |
|---|---|
| **la correspondance** | connection |
| **une étiquette** | label |
| **la sonnette d'alarme** | alarm, communication cord |
| **la station de métro** | underground or subway station |

*** LE CHEMIN DE FER

| | |
|---|---|
| **la banquette** | seat |
| **la carte d'abonnement** | season ticket |
| **la locomotive** | locomotive, engine |
| **la malle** | trunk |
| **la salle des pas perdus** | waiting room |
| **la station de taxis** | taxi rank |

**attraper/manquer sa correspondance** to catch/miss one's connection

**sonner l'alarme** to pull the communication cord

## LES COULEURS (fpl)

| | |
|---|---|
| **beige** | beige |
| **blanc (blanche)** | white |
| **bleu\* (bleue)** | blue |
| **brun (brune)** | brown |
| **fauve** | fawn, tawny |
| **gris (grise)** | grey |
| **jaune** | yellow |
| **marron\*** | brown |
| **noir (noire)** | black |
| **orange, orangé** | orange |
| **pourpre** | crimson |
| **rose\*** | pink |
| **rosé** | rosé |
| **rouge** | red |
| **vert (verte)** | green |
| **violet (violette)** | violet, purple |
| | |
| **bleu clair** | pale blue |
| **bleu foncé** | dark blue |
| **bleuâtre, bleuté** | bluish |
| | |
| **bleu ciel** | sky blue |
| **bleu marine** | navy blue |
| **bleu roi** | royal blue |

**le bleu lui va bien** blue suits him (or her)
**peindre quelque chose en bleu** to paint something
   blue

## LES COULEURS

**changer de couleur** to change colour
**la Maison Blanche** the White House
**un Blanc** a white man
**une Blanche** a white woman
**blanc comme la neige** as white as snow
**Blanche-Neige** Snow-White
**un steak bleu** a very rare steak, an underdone steak
**le Petit Chaperon Rouge** Little Red Riding Hood
**rougir** to turn red
**rougir de honte/de gêne** to blush with shame/with
  embarrassment
**pâle comme un linge** as white as a sheet
**bleu de froid** blue with cold
**tous les trente-six du mois** once in a blue moon
**elle brunit** she is turning brown
**les feuilles roussissent** the leaves are turning brown
**tout(e) bronzé(e)** as brown as a berry
**il était couvert de bleus** he was black and blue
**un Noir** a black man
**une Noire** a black woman
**un œil poché, un œil au beurre noir** a black eye
**vert(e) de jalousie** green with envy
**il a le pouce vert** he's got green fingers

**\* LA DESCRIPTION DES GENS**

| | |
|---|---|
| **l'âge** | age |
| **un air\*** | appearance |
| **le bouton\*** | spot, pimple |
| **les cheveux** | hair |

**quel âge avez-vous?** how old are you?, what age are you?

**j'ai 16 ans** I am 16 (years old)

**un homme d'un certain âge** a middle-aged man

**avoir l'air de s'ennuyer** to look bored, seem bored

**elle a l'air d'une enfant** she looks like a child

**il/elle a l'air triste** he/she looks sad

**il/elle a l'air sympathique** he/she looks nice or pleasant or friendly

**il/elle a l'air fatigué/fatigué(e)** he/she looks tired

**il/elle a l'air intelligent/intelligent(e)** he/she looks intelligent

**avoir des boutons** to have spots or pimples, have a pimply face

**être chauve** to be bald

**avoir les cheveux blonds** to have blond or fair hair

**les cheveux bouclés** curly hair

**les cheveux bruns** dark or brown hair

**les cheveux châtains** chestnut hair

**les cheveux frisés** curly hair

**les cheveux ondulés** wavy hair

**les cheveux roux** red hair

**les cheveux teints** dyed hair

**\* LA DESCRIPTION DES GENS**

| | |
|---|---|
| **la barbe** | beard |
| **la:honte** | shame |
| **la larme** | tear |
| **les lunettes** | glasses |
| **la moustache** | moustache |
| **la taille\*** | height, size; waist |

**barbu** bearded

**avoir honte/peur de faire quelque chose** to be ashamed/afraid of doing something

**en larmes** in tears

**au bord des larmes** on the verge of tears

**avoir les larmes aux yeux** to have tears in one's eyes

**des larmes de joie/de colère** tears of joy/rage

**des larmes de crocodile** crocodile tears

**porter des lunettes** to wear glasses

**porter la moustache, porter des moustaches** to have a moustache

**un homme de taille moyenne** a man of average height

**un homme de petite taille** a short man

**un homme de grande taille** a tall man

**elle doit faire 1 mètre 70 (de taille)** she must be 1 metre 70 tall

**les grandes/petites tailles** the large/small sizes

**avoir la taille fine** to have a slim waist

**prendre quelqu'un par la taille** to put one's arm round somebody's waist

## ** LA DESCRIPTION DES GENS

| | |
|---|---|
| le caractère | character, nature |
| le défaut | fault, bad quality |
| le geste | movement, gesture |
| le teint | complexion, colouring |
| le trait | feature |
| les verres (de contact) | contact lenses |

**avoir bon caractère** to be good-natured *or* good-tempered

**avoir mauvais caractère** to be ill-natured *or* bad-tempered

**faire un geste de la main** to gesture with one's hand, give a wave (of one's hand)

**avoir le teint jaune/pâle** to have a sallow/pale complexion

**avoir le teint frais** to have a fresh complexion

**avoir le teint bronzé** to be tanned

**avoir des traits fins** to have delicate features

**avoir les traits tirés** to look drawn

**un trait de génie** a brainwave

**les verres fumés** tinted lenses

## ** LA DESCRIPTION DES GENS

| | |
|---|---|
| l'allure | walk, gait |
| la beauté | beauty |
| la cicatrice | scar |
| la conscience | conscience |
| une expression | expression |
| la frange | fringe |
| l'habitude | habit |
| l'humeur | mood, humour |
| la laideur | ugliness |
| les lentilles | contact lenses |
| la qualité | (good) quality |
| la ressemblance | resemblance, similarity |
| la ride | wrinkle |

avoir une drôle d'allure, avoir un drôle d'air to
   look odd or funny
il a fait une drôle de tête! you should have seen
   his face!
avoir bonne/mauvaise conscience to have a clear/
   bad conscience
avoir l'habitude de faire to be in the habit of doing
beau/belle handsome/beautiful
laid/laide ugly
laid/laide à faire peur frightfully ugly
être de bonne humeur to be in a good mood or
   humour
être de mauvaise humeur to be in a bad mood
un double menton a double chin
il ressemble à son père he looks like his father, he
   resembles his father
il a une certaine ressemblance avec son père he has
   a certain resemblance to his father
il y a une certaine ressemblance entre . . . there is a
   certain resemblance between . . .
une figure ridée a wrinkled face
être en colère (contre quelqu'un) to be angry
   (with somebody)
se mettre en colère to get angry
se ronger les ongles to bite one's nails

\*\*\* LA DESCRIPTION DES GENS

| | |
|---|---|
| **le dentier** | (set of) false teeth |
| **le géant** | giant |
| **le grain de beauté** | beauty spot |
| **le nain** | dwarf |

**l'homme aux yeux bleus** the man with blue eyes
**avoir les yeux enfoncés** to have deepset eyes
**avoir les yeux marron** to have brown eyes
**avoir les yeux noisette** to have hazel eyes
**être myope/hypermétrope** to be short-sighted/long-sighted
**être au désespoir** to be in despair

**aveugle** blind
**boiteux/boiteuse** lame
**bossu/bossue** hunch-backed
**gauche** clumsy, awkward
**maladroit/maladroite** clumsy
**muet/muette** dumb
**sourd/sourde** deaf

*** LA DESCRIPTION DES GENS

| | |
|---|---|
| la boucle | curl |
| la fossette | dimple |
| la permanente | perm |
| la sueur | sweat |
| la tache de rousseur, | |
| la tache de son | freckle |
| la timidité | shyness, timidity |

**assis/assise** sitting, seated
**basané/basanée** sunburned
**charmant/charmante** charming
**clair/claire** fair (*of skin*), light
**debout** standing (up)
**droitier/droitière** right-handed
**dur/dure** hard, harsh
**étroit/étroite** narrow
**faible** weak
**foncé/foncée** deep, dark (*of colour*)
**gai/gaie** gay, merry
**gaucher/gauchère** left-handed
**grand/grande** big, tall
**gras/grasse, gros/grosse** fat, stout
**long/longue** long
**maigre** thin, skinny
**mat/mate** sallow
**méchant/méchante** naughty
**mince** slim, slender
**moyen/moyenne** average
**petit/petite** small
**pointu/pointue** pointed
**raide** straight
**ravissant/ravissante** delightful
**rond/ronde** round
**soigné/soignée** neat, well-groomed
**svelte** slim, slender
**sympathique** nice, pleasant, friendly
**timide** shy
**trapu/trapue** thickset
**vilain/vilaine** ugly, nasty

**\* L'ENSEIGNEMENT**

| | |
|---|---|
| l'allemand | German |
| un ami | friend |
| l'anglais | English |
| le cahier | exercise book, jotter |
| le camarade (de classe) | (school) friend |
| le carnet | notebook |
| le cartable | satchel |
| le chant | singing |
| le collège | secondary school |
| le collège technique | technical college |
| le collégien | college student |
| le copain | pal |
| le couloir | corridor |
| les cours | lessons |
| le couvent | convent; convent school |
| le crayon | pencil |
| le dessin | (*subject*) art, drawing; (*piece of work*) drawing |
| les devoirs | homework |
| le dictionnaire | dictionary |
| un écolier | schoolboy |
| un élève | pupil, schoolboy |
| un emploi du temps | timetable |
| l'espagnol | Spanish |
| un étudiant | student |
| un examen | exam, examination |
| un exercice | exercise |
| le français | French |
| un instituteur | primary schoolteacher |
| le jour de congé | day off, holiday |
| le laboratoire (de langues) | (language) laboratory |
| le latin | Latin |
| le livre | book |
| le lycée | secondary school |
| le lycéen | secondary school pupil |
| le magnétophone | tape recorder |
| le papier | paper |
| le personnel | staff |

**\* L'ENSEIGNEMENT**

| | |
|---|---|
| une amie | friend |
| l'arithmétique | arithmetic |
| la camarade (de classe) | (school) friend |
| la carte* | map |
| la classe | class |
| la collégienne | college student |
| la conférence | lecture |
| la copine | pal |
| la cour | playground |
| la craie | chalk |
| une école (primaire) | primary school |
| l'éducation | education |
| une élève | pupil, schoolgirl |
| l'encre | ink |
| une erreur | error |
| l'étude (de) | study (of) |
| les études | studies |
| une étudiante | student |
| la faute* | mistake |
| la géographie | geography |
| la gomme | rubber |
| les grandes vacances | summer holidays |
| l'histoire* | history; story |
| une institutrice | primary schoolteacher |
| la leçon (de français) | (French) lesson |
| la lecture | reading |
| la lycéenne | secondary school pupil |
| les mathématiques, les math(s) | mathematics, maths |
| la musique | music |
| la note* | mark |
| la plume* | pen |
| la question | question |
| la règle* | rule; ruler |
| la rentrée (des classes) | beginning of term |
| la sacoche* | schoolbag, satchel |
| la salle de classe | classroom |

## * L'ENSEIGNEMENT (*suite*)

| | |
|---|---|
| le prix* | prize |
| le professeur | secondary (school) teacher |
| les progrès | progress |
| le pupitre | desk |
| le résultat | result |
| le stylo (à encre) | fountain pen |
| le stylo à bille | ballpoint pen |
| le succès | success |
| le tableau (noir) | blackboard |
| le test | test |
| le torchon* | duster |

apprendre quelque chose par cœur to learn something by heart
aller à l'école (*or* au lycée *etc*) to go to school
quitter l'école (*or* le lycée *etc*) to leave school
enseigner le français to teach French
faire ses devoirs to do one's homework
avoir congé le mercredi to have Wednesdays off
gagner un prix to win a prize
le professeur d'allemand the German teacher
faire des progrès to make progress
il nous fait passer un test he gives us a test
essuyer le tableau noir to wipe the blackboard
écrire au tableau noir/dans son cahier to write on the blackboard/in one's jotter
passer un examen to sit an exam
être reçu à un examen, réussir à un examen to pass an exam
échouer à un examen, rater un examen to fail an exam
un élève sérieux/dissipé a serious/an unruly pupil

---

\* **L'ENSEIGNEMENT** (*suite*)
| | |
|---|---|
| **la serviette**\* | briefcase |
| **l'université** | university |
| **les vacances** | holidays |

**effacer une erreur** to rub out an error
**pendant les grandes vacances** during the summer holidays
**à la rentrée des classes** at the beginning of term
**étudier les langues modernes** to study modern languages
**avoir une bonne note** to get a good mark *or* good marks
**avoir la moyenne** to get fifty per cent *or* half marks
**l'année scolaire** the school year
**repasser une leçon** to go over a lesson again
**repasser ses leçons, réviser** to revise
**corriger** to correct
**taisez-vous!** be quiet!
**faire l'école buissonnière** to play truant

## ** L'ENSEIGNEMENT

| | |
|---|---|
| les arts ménagers | domestic science, homecraft |
| le baccalauréat, le bac*, le bachot | French school-leaving certificate |
| le bic | ballpoint pen |
| le bulletin | report |
| le concours* | competitive exam |
| le diplôme | diploma |
| le dortoir | dormitory |
| l'enseignement | education, teaching |
| le feutre | felt-tip pen |
| l'italien | Italian |
| le moniteur | monitor, prefect |
| le proviseur | headmaster (of lycée) |
| le rang | row (of seats etc) |
| le stylo feutre | felt-tip pen |
| le trimestre | term |
| le vestiaire | cloakroom |
| le vocabulaire | vocabulary |

**préparer son bac** to be sitting one's A-levels or Highers or school-leaving certificate
**au troisième rang** in the third row

## ** L'ENSEIGNEMENT

| | |
|---|---|
| l'algèbre | algebra |
| la chimie | chemistry |
| la classe terminale | final year |
| la composition | composition, essay; class exam |
| la couture | needlework |
| la dictée | dictation |
| une école maternelle | nursery school |
| une école mixte | mixed school, co-ed |
| une école normale | College of Education |
| l'éducation physique | physical education, P.E. |
| une épreuve | test |
| la géométrie | geometry |
| la grammaire | grammar |
| la gymnastique | gym |
| l'histoire naturelle, les sciences naturelles | biology, natural history |
| l'instruction religieuse | religious instruction |
| les langues* modernes | (modern) languages |
| la matière | (school) subject |
| la monitrice | monitor, prefect |
| la moyenne | fifty per cent, half marks; pass, passmark |
| la phrase | sentence |
| la physique | physics |
| la punition | punishment |
| la récréation | break, interval |

en terminale in the top class
en sixième in first year, in the first form
en première in sixth year, in the sixth form

\*\*\* L'ENSEIGNEMENT

| | |
|---|---|
| un absent | absentee |
| le bouquin | book (*informal*) |
| le brouillon | rough copy |
| le demi-pensionnaire | day-boy |
| le directeur | headmaster |
| l'examinateur | examiner |
| un externe | day-boy |
| le grec | Greek |
| un internat | boarding school |
| un interne | boarder |
| le papier buvard | blotting paper |
| le pâté\* | (ink) blot |
| le pensionnaire\* | boarder |
| le principal | headmaster (*of college*) |
| le réfectoire | dining hall, canteen |
| le règlement | rule |
| le russe | Russian |
| le stylomine | propelling pencil |
| le taille-crayon (*pl* taille-crayons)* | pencil sharpener |
| le thème | prose translation (*into a foreign language*) |

punir un **élève** to punish a pupil
l'**élève** (*mf*) de terminale chargé(e) d'un certain
nombre de responsabilités head boy/girl

**\*\*\* L'ENSEIGNEMENT**

| | |
|---|---|
| une absence | absence |
| une absente | absentee |
| la cantine | dining hall, canteen |
| la colle* | detention |
| la conduite | behaviour |
| la directrice | headmistress |
| la distribution des prix | prize-giving |
| l'écriture | handwriting |
| une externe | day-girl |
| la faculté, la fac | university |
| la feuille de présence | absence sheet |
| une interne | boarder |
| la machine à calculer | calculator |
| la menuiserie | woodwork |
| l'orthographe | spelling |
| la poésie | poetry |
| la retenue | detention |
| la tache | blot |
| la tâche | task |
| la traduction | translation (*technique, exercise*) |
| la version | (unseen) translation (*from a foreign language*) |

en l'absence du professeur in the teacher's absence,
  while the teacher was away (*or* is away)
manger à la cantine to have school meals
mettre une colle à quelqu'un to give somebody
  detention, keep somebody in
j'ai eu 3 heures de colle I was kept in for 3 hours
il nous met en retenue he puts us in detention, he
  keeps us in
aller à l'université *or* à la fac to go to university
obtenir sa licence to graduate (from university)

## * LA FAMILLE

| | |
|---|---|
| l'âge | age |
| le bébé | baby |
| le couple | couple |
| le cousin | cousin |
| un enfant | child |
| le fils [fis] | son |
| le frère | brother |
| le garçon* | boy |
| le grand-père | grandfather |
| le jeune homme | youth, young man |
| le mari | husband |
| le nom | name |
| le marié | bridegroom |
| les nouveaux mariés | newly-weds |
| un oncle | uncle |
| le parent* | parent; relation, relative |
| les parents* | parents; relations, relatives |
| le père | father |
| le petit-fils [pətifis] (pl petits-fils) | grandson |
| les petits-enfants [pətizᾶfᾶ] | grandchildren |
| le vieillard | old man |
| le voisin | neighbour |

le même âge que the same age as
plus âgé que older than
plus jeune que younger than
papa! Daddy!
le bébé grandit the baby is growing
mon père vieillit my father is getting old
les jeunes, les jeunes gens young people
nom de jeune fille maiden name
appeler un enfant **Paul** to call a child Paul
comment s'appelle-t-il? what is his name?, what
  is he called?
je m'appelle **Robert** my name is Robert

\* LA FAMILLE

| | |
|---|---|
| la cousine | cousin |
| une enfant | child |
| la famille | family |
| la femme\* | woman; wife |
| la fille | daughter |
| la fillette | (young) girl |
| les gens | people |
| la grand'mère | grandmother |
| la jeune fille | girl |
| la jeune mariée | bride |
| la mère | mother |
| la personne | person; (*in plural*) people |
| la petite-fille | grand-daughter |
| la sœur | sister |
| la tante | aunt |
| la voisine | neighbour |

maman! Mummy!
faire la connaissance de quelqu'un to meet somebody, to get to know somebody
en famille with the family; as a family
les enfants dépendent de leurs parents children are dependent on their parents
qui est le chef de famille? who is the head of the family?
la famille s'agrandit the family is growing

## ** LA FAMILLE

| | |
|---|---|
| les adultes | adults |
| l'aîné | elder, eldest |
| le cadet | younger, youngest |
| l'époux | husband, spouse |
| le fiancé | fiancé |
| le gosse | kid |
| les jumeaux | twins |
| le neveu | nephew |
| le nom de famille | surname |
| le prénom | first name, Christian name |

## *** LA FAMILLE

| | |
|---|---|
| un ancêtre | ancestor |
| le beau-fils [bofis] | son-in-law |
| le beau-frère | brother-in-law |
| le beau-père | father-in-law; step-father |
| le célibataire (endurci) | (confirmed) bachelor |
| le demi-frère | step-brother |
| le gendre | son-in-law |
| un orphelin | orphan |
| un orphelinat | orphanage |
| le parrain | godfather |
| le retraité | (old age) pensioner |
| le surnom | nickname |
| les triplés | triplets |
| le tuteur | guardian |
| le veuf | widower |

se marier avec quelqu'un to marry somebody
se remarier to remarry
un arbre généalogique family tree
avec mon frère jumeau with my twin brother
donner le biberon à un bébé to give a baby its bottle
son fils/sa fille unique his (or her) only son/daughter
mon oncle est veuf/est retraité my uncle is a widower/an old age pensioner

**\*\* LA FAMILLE**

| | |
|---|---|
| l'aînée | elder, eldest |
| la cadette | younger, youngest |
| une épouse | wife, spouse |
| la fiancée | fiancée |
| la gosse | kid |
| les grandes personnes | grown-ups |
| la jeunesse | youth (*stage of life*) |
| les jumelles\* | twins, twin sisters |
| la ménagère | housewife |
| la nièce | niece |
| la vieillesse | old age |

**\*\*\* LA FAMILLE**

| | |
|---|---|
| la belle-fille, la bru | daughter-in-law |
| la belle-mère | mother-in-law; step-mother |
| la belle-sœur | sister-in-law |
| la célibataire | spinster |
| la demi-sœur | step-sister |
| la marraine | godmother |
| une orpheline | orphan |
| la retraitée | (old age) pensioner |
| la veuve | widow |

**dans ma jeunesse** in my youth, when I was young
**des livres pour la jeunesse** books for young people
**ma mère travaille au dehors** my mother goes out to work
**avec ma sœur jumelle** with my twin sister
**une mère qui abandonne ses enfants** a mother who abandons her children
**les enfants martyrs** battered babies
**chez les Smith** at the Smiths'
**ma tante est veuve/est retraitée** my aunt is a widow/an old age pensioner

**\* LA FERME**

| | |
|---|---|
| un animal | |
| (*pl* animaux) | animal |
| le bœuf\* [bœf] (*pl* -s [bø]) | ox |
| le canard | duck |
| le champ | field |
| le chat | cat |
| le cheval (*pl* chevaux) | horse |
| le chien | dog |
| le cochon | pig |
| le coq | cock |
| le fermier | farmer |
| le grenier\* | loft |
| le moulin (à vent) | (wind)mill |
| le mouton\* | sheep |
| le pays\* | country; district |
| le poulet | chicken |
| le ruisseau (*pl* -x) | stream |
| le veau\* (*pl* -x) | calf |
| le village | village |

**\*\* LA FERME**

| | |
|---|---|
| un âne | donkey |
| un étang | pond |
| le foin | hay |
| le fossé | ditch |
| le grain | grain, seed |
| le paysan | country person, peasant |
| le sol | ground, earth, land |
| le tas | heap, pile |
| le taureau (*pl* -x) | bull |
| le tracteur | tractor |

**le cheval de trait** cart-horse
**le chien de berger** sheep-dog

**\* LA FERME**

| | |
|---|---|
| la barrière\* | gate |
| la boue | mud |
| la camionnette | (small) van |
| à la campagne | in the country; to the country |
| la charrette | cart |
| la chèvre | goat |
| la colline | hill |
| une échelle | ladder |
| la ferme | farm, farmhouse |
| la fermière | farmer's wife |
| la forêt | forest |
| une oie | goose |
| la poule | hen |
| la terre | earth, ground |
| la vache | cow |

**\*\* LA FERME**

| | |
|---|---|
| l'avoine | oats |
| la mare | pond |
| la meule de foin | haystack |
| la moisson | harvest |
| la paille | straw |
| la paysanne | country woman, peasant |
| la poussière | dust |
| la récolte | crop |
| la vigne | vine |

**travailler dans une ferme** to work on a farm

### *** LA FERME

| | |
|---|---|
| un agneau (*pl* -x) | lamb |
| le bélier | ram |
| le berger | shepherd |
| le bétail | cattle |
| le blé | corn; wheat |
| le chevreau (*pl* -x) | kid |
| le dindon | turkey |
| un épouvantail | scarecrow |
| le fumier | manure |
| le hangar | shed, barn |
| le laboureur | ploughman |
| le maïs [ma-is] | maize |
| le porc* | pig |
| le poulailler* | henhouse, hen coop |
| le poulain | foal |
| le poussin | chick, chicken |
| le pré | meadow |
| le puits | well |
| le seau (*pl* -x) | bucket, pail |
| le seigle | rye |
| le sillon | furrow |
| le tombereau (*pl* -x) | tipcart |
| le troupeau (*pl* -x) | (*sheep*) flock; (*cattle*) herd |

**traire les vaches** to milk the cows
**ramasser les œufs** to gather the eggs
**donner à manger aux poules** to feed the hens
**labourer les champs** to plough the fields
**rentrer la moisson, faire la récolte** to bring in the harvest, bring in the crops

### *** LA FERME

| | |
|---|---|
| la baratte | churn |
| la basse-cour | farmyard |
| la céréale | cereal crop |
| la charrue | plough |
| la chaumière | (thatched) cottage |
| une écurie | stable |
| une étable | cow-shed, byre |
| la fièvre aphteuse | foot and mouth disease |
| la gerbe | sheaf |
| la grange | barn |
| la lande | moor, heath |
| la moissonneuse-<br>batteuse | combine harvester |
| l'orge | barley |
| la palissade | fence |
| la porcherie | pigsty |

## * LES FRUITS ET LES ARBRES FRUITIERS

| | |
|---|---|
| un ananas | pineapple |
| un arbre fruitier | fruit tree |
| le citron | lemon |
| un fruit | a piece of fruit, some fruit |
| les fruits | fruit |
| le pommier | apple tree |

## ** LES FRUITS ET LES ARBRES FRUITIERS

| | |
|---|---|
| un abricot | apricot |
| le bananier | banana tree |
| le citronnier | lemon tree |
| le marron (grillé) | (roasted) chestnut |
| l'oranger | orange tree |
| le pamplemousse | grapefruit |
| le pêcher | peach tree |
| le poirier | pear tree |
| le raisin | grape(s) |
| le verger | orchard |
| le vignoble | vineyard |

## *** LES FRUITS ET LES ARBRES FRUITIERS

| | |
|---|---|
| un abricotier | apricot tree |
| un avocat* | avocado pear |
| le cassis | blackcurrant; blackcurrant bush |
| le cerisier | cherry tree |
| le dattier | date palm |
| le figuier | fig tree |
| le fraisier | strawberry plant |
| le framboisier | raspberry bush or cane |
| le groseillier | redcurrant bush |
| le groseillier à maquereau | gooseberry bush |
| le noisetier | hazel tree |
| le noyau (pl -x) | stone (in fruit) |
| le noyer | walnut tree |
| le pépin | pip (in fruit) |
| le pruneau (pl -x) | prune |
| le prunier | plum tree |

### * LES FRUITS ET LES ARBRES FRUITIERS

| | |
|---|---|
| la **banane** | banana |
| la **fraise** | strawberry |
| la **framboise** | raspberry |
| une **orange** | orange |
| la **pêche**\* | peach |
| la **peau** | skin |
| la **poire** | pear |
| la **pomme** | apple |
| la **tomate** | tomato; tomato plant |

### ** LES FRUITS ET LES ARBRES FRUITIERS

| | |
|---|---|
| la **cerise** | cherry |
| la **vigne** | vine |

### *** LES FRUITS ET LES ARBRES FRUITIERS

| | |
|---|---|
| la **baie**\* | berry |
| la **datte** | date |
| la **figue** | fig |
| la **grenade** | pomegranate |
| la **groseille** | redcurrant |
| la **groseille à maquereau** | gooseberry |
| la **mûre** | blackberry, bramble |
| la **myrtille** | bilberry |
| la **noisette** | hazelnut |
| la **noix** | nut; walnut |
| la **prune** | plum |
| la **rhubarbe** | rhubarb |

un **jus d'ananas/de pamplemousse** a pineapple/
grapefruit juice
un **citron pressé** a (fresh) lemon drink
une **grappe de raisin** a bunch of grapes
le **raisin sec** raisin; le **raisin sec de Smyrne** sultana;
le **raisin de Corinthe** currant
**mordre (dans) une pomme** to bite (into) an apple
une **tarte aux pommes/à la rhubarbe** apple/rhubarb
tart
**mûrir** to ripen; **mûr** ripe; **pas mûr** unripe
**gâté, pourri** rotten; **éplucher** to peel

## * L'HEURE

| | |
|---|---|
| **un an** | year |
| **un après-midi** | afternoon |
| **un instant** | moment |
| **le jour** | day |
| **le matin** | morning |
| **à midi** | at mid-day, at noon |
| **à minuit** | at midnight |
| **le mois** | month |
| **le moment** | moment |
| **le quart d'heure** | quarter of an hour |
| **le siècle** | century; age |
| **le soir** | evening |
| **le temps*** | time |
| **après-demain** | the day after tomorrow |
| **aujourd'hui** | today |
| **avant-hier** | the day before yesterday |
| **demain** | tomorrow |
| **hier** | yesterday |

**il a 22 ans** he is 22 (years old)
**il y a 2 jours** 2 days ago
**dans 2 jours** in 2 days, in 2 days' time
**huit jours** a week; **quinze jours** a fortnight
**tous les jours** every day
**de nos jours** these days, nowadays, in this day and
age
**quel jour sommes-nous aujourd'hui?** what day is it
today?
**c'est le combien?, le combien sommes-nous?** what's
the date?
**au mois de janvier** in (the month of) January
**en ce moment** at the moment, at present, just now
**à ce moment là** at that (very) moment
**3 heures moins le quart** (a) quarter to 3
**3 heures et quart** (a) quarter past 3
**hier soir** last night, yesterday evening
**de temps en temps** from time to time
**je n'ai pas le temps de vous voir** I don't have the
time to see you

# * L'HEURE

| | |
|---|---|
| une année | a (whole) year |
| une après-midi | a (whole) afternoon |
| la date | date |
| une demi-heure | half an hour, a half-hour |
| la fois | time, occasion |
| l'heure | time (in general) |
| une heure | hour |
| la journée | the (whole) day |
| la matinée | the (whole) morning |
| la minute | minute |
| la montre | watch |
| la nuit | night |
| la seconde | second |
| la semaine | week |
| la soirée | the (whole) evening |

l'année dernière/prochaine last/next year

chaque année every year

quelle est la date d'aujourd'hui? what is today's date?

une fois/deux fois/trois fois once/twice/three times

plusieurs fois several times, a number of times

3 fois par an 3 times a year

9 fois sur 10 9 times out of 10

il était une fois, il y avait une fois once upon a time there was

à la fois at once, at the same time

quelle heure est-il? what time is it?, what is the time?

avez-vous l'heure (exacte or juste)? have you got the (right) time?

il est 6 heures/6 heures 10/6 heures moins 10/6 heures et demie it is 6 (o'clock)/10 past 6/10 to 6/half past 6

tout à l'heure (recent past) a short while ago, just now; (near future) in a little while, shortly

tôt, de bonne heure early; tard late

## ** L'HEURE

| | |
|---|---|
| l'avenir | future |
| le calendrier | calendar |
| le futur | future; the future tense |
| le lendemain | the next day, the day after |
| le passé | the past; the past tense |
| le présent | the present (time); the present tense |
| le retard | delay; lateness |
| le surlendemain | two days later, the day after (that) |
| le week-end | weekend |

## *** L'HEURE

| | |
|---|---|
| le cadran | face (of clock etc), dial |
| le chronomètre | stopwatch |
| un intervalle | interval (of time) |
| le réveil, le réveille-matin | alarm clock |

à l'avenir in (the) future
à l'instant (présent) at this very instant or minute
le jour de congé day off, holiday
le jour férié public holiday, bank holiday
le jour ouvrable weekday
par un jour de pluie on a rainy day, one rainy day
au lever du jour at dawn, at daybreak
le lendemain matin/soir the next or following morning/evening
à présent at present, now; nowadays
cette montre retarde/avance this watch is slow/fast
vous êtes en retard you're late
au vingtième siècle in the twentieth century
le cours du soir evening class
il passe tout son temps à travailler he spends all his time working
le temps passe or s'écoule time passes
à temps in time

## ** L'HEURE

| | |
|---|---|
| l'heure du dîner | dinner time |
| une horloge | (large) clock |
| la pendule | clock |
| la veille | the day before |

### *** L'HEURE

| | |
|---|---|
| une aiguille* | hand (of clock etc) |
| une année bissextile | leap year |
| l'avant-veille | two days before or previously |
| la décennie | decade |
| une époque | epoch; (particular) time |
| une horloge normande | grandfather clock |
| la pendule à coucou | cuckoo clock |
| la quinzaine | fortnight |

avancer/retarder l'horloge to put the clock forward/back

faire la grasse matinée to have a long lie, have a lie-in

d'une minute à l'autre any minute now

il est 2 heures à ma montre it is 2 o'clock by my watch

cette nuit (already past) last night; (still to come) tonight

souhaiter (une) bonne nuit à quelqu'un to wish somebody goodnight

à la tombée de la nuit at nightfall

l'avant-dernière semaine the week before last

la veille de Noël (on) Christmas Eve

la veille au soir the previous evening, the night or evening before

---

**\* L'HÔTEL**

| | |
|---|---|
| un ascenseur | lift |
| un aubergiste | innkeeper |
| les bagages | luggage |
| le bar | bar |
| le chef\* (de cuisine) | chef, head cook |
| le client\* | resident, guest |
| un étage | floor, storey |
| le garçon\* | waiter |
| l'hôte\* | host; guest |
| l'hôtel\* | hotel |
| un invité | guest |
| le porteur | porter |
| le pourboire | tip |
| le réceptionniste | receptionist, reception clerk |
| le restaurant | restaurant |
| le service | service; service charge |
| le téléviseur (couleur) | (colour) television |

**faire monter/faire descendre ses bagages** to have one's luggage taken up/taken down

**monter ses bagages à sa chambre** to take up one's luggage to one's room

**descendre ses bagages de sa chambre** to take down one's luggage from one's room

**au premier étage** on the first floor

**garçon!** waiter!; **mademoiselle!** waitress!, excuse me miss!

**le chef fait la cuisine** the chef does the cooking

**'service compris'** 'service included'

## * L'HÔTEL

| | |
|---|---|
| une addition | bill |
| une auberge | inn |
| une aubergiste | innkeeper; innkeeper's wife |
| la chambre | room |
| la cliente* | resident, guest |
| la douche | shower |
| une hôtesse | host, hostess |
| une invitée | guest |
| la (petite) monnaie | (small) change |
| la piscine | swimming pool |
| la réception | reception (desk) |
| la réceptionniste | receptionist |
| la salle de bains | bathroom |
| la salle à manger | dining room |
| la valise | case, suitcase |
| la vue | view |

louer *or* réserver une chambre dans un hôtel to book a room in a hôtel
c'est combien? how much is it?
une chambre avec douche/avec salle de bains a room with a shower/with private bathroom

## ** L'HÔTEL

| | |
|---|---|
| le balcon* | balcony |
| le bureau de réception | reception (desk) |
| le cabinet de toilette | toilet |
| le chasseur* | page(-boy) |
| le foyer | foyer |
| le grand lit | double bed |
| un hôtelier | hotel-keeper |
| le patron* | boarding-house proprietor |

## *** L'HÔTEL

| | |
|---|---|
| le cabaret | 'pub' |
| le cuisinier | cook |
| un estaminet | 'pub' |
| le maître d'hôtel | head waiter |
| le pensionnaire* | resident, guest (at boarding house) |
| le sommelier | wine waiter |
| le tarif | scale of charges, tariff |

s'inscrire sur le registre to register
remplir une fiche to fill in a form
une chambre avec un lit pour deux personnes a double room
une chambre à deux lits a twin-bedded room
une chambre à une personne a single room
la chambre donne sur la plage the room overlooks the beach

## ** L'HÔTEL

| | |
|---|---|
| la femme de chambre | chamber maid |
| une hôtelière | hotel-keeper |
| la note* | bill |
| la patronne* | boarding-house proprietor |
| la pension | (building) guest-house, boarding house; (type of facilities) full board |
| la pension de famille | guest-house, boarding house, private hotel |
| la salle de télévision | television lounge |
| la serveuse | waitress |
| la terrasse | terrace, pavement outside a café |
| les toilettes | toilets, 'ladies', 'gents' |

## *** L'HÔTEL

| | |
|---|---|
| la pensionnaire* | resident, guest (at boarding house) |
| la sortie de secours | fire escape |

chambre sans pension room (with no meals)
chambre avec demi-pension room with breakfast and dinner provided
chambre avec pension complète room and full board
la femme de chambre fait les lits et nettoie la chambre the chamber maid makes the beds and cleans the rooms
la serveuse nous sert à la terrasse the waitress serves us outside on the terrace
'vous n'avez qu'à sonner' 'just ring'

## * LES INSTRUMENTS DE MUSIQUE

| | |
|---|---|
| un accordéon | accordion |
| un instrument de musique | musical instrument |
| le jazz [dʒɑz] | jazz |
| un orchestre* | orchestra |
| le piano | piano |

## ** LES INSTRUMENTS DE MUSIQUE

| | |
|---|---|
| le bâton* | conductor's baton |
| le chef d'orchestre | conductor |
| le musicien | musician |
| le tambour | drum |
| le violon | violin, fiddle |

## *** LES INSTRUMENTS DE MUSIQUE

| | |
|---|---|
| un accord* | chord |
| le basson | bassoon |
| le clairon | bugle |
| le cor d'harmonie | French horn |
| l'harmonica | harmonica, mouth organ |
| le :hautbois | oboe |
| un orgue | organ |
| le saxophone | saxophone |
| le soliste | soloist |
| le tambourin | tambourine |
| le triangle | triangle |
| le trombone | trombone |
| le violoncelle | cello |
| le xylophone [ksilɔfɔn] | xylophone |

écouter la musique to listen to the music
jouer du piano/de la guitare/du violon to play the piano/the guitar/the violin
le chef d'orchestre conduit l'orchestre the conductor conducts the orchestra
le premier violon conduit the first violin leads
le piano à queue, le piano de concert grand piano

## * LES INSTRUMENTS DE MUSIQUE

| | |
|---|---|
| la guitare | guitar |
| la musique | music |
| la salle des fêtes, | |
| la salle de concert | concert hall |
| la trompette | trumpet |

## ** LES INSTRUMENTS DE MUSIQUE

| | |
|---|---|
| la corde* | string |
| les cymbales | cymbals |
| la flûte | flute |
| la flûte à bec | recorder |
| la :harpe | harp |
| la note* | note |

## *** LES INSTRUMENTS DE MUSIQUE

| | |
|---|---|
| la clarinette | clarinet |
| la contrebasse | double bass |
| la cornemuse | bagpipes |
| la fanfare* | brass band |
| la grosse caisse | big drum, bass drum |
| la soliste | soloist |
| la touche* | (piano) key |

chanter ses propres louanges to blow one's own trumpet
jouer de la batterie to play the drums
travailler son piano to practise the piano
les cordes, les instruments à cordes the strings, the strings section
les vents, les instruments à vent the wind instruments
les bois the woodwind section
les instruments à percussion the percussion instruments
jouer or interpréter un morceau to play a piece
une fausse note a wrong note
jouer juste/faux to play in tune/out of tune, play in key/out of key

**\* LE JARDIN ET LES FLEURS**

| | |
|---|---|
| **un arbre** | tree |
| **le bouquet de fleurs** | bunch of flowers |
| **le bouton-d'or** (*pl* **boutons-d'or**) | buttercup |
| **le buisson** | bush |
| **le gazon** | lawn; turf |
| **le jardin** | garden |
| **le jardinage** | gardening |
| **le jardinier** | gardener |
| **les légumes** | vegetables |
| **le papillon** | butterfly |
| **le parfum** | perfume, scent |
| **le rosier** | rose bush |
| **le rouleau** (*pl* **-x**) | (garden) roller |
| **le sol** | earth, soil |
| **le tronc** | trunk |
| **le verger** | orchard |

**ça sent bon!** that smells nice!
**le jardin est entouré d'une haie** the garden is surrounded by a hedge
**bêcher le jardin** to dig the garden
**tondre le gazon** to mow the lawn

## * LE JARDIN ET LES FLEURS

| | |
|---|---|
| une abeille | bee |
| la **barrière*** | gate |
| la **branche** | branch |
| une échelle | ladder |
| la **feuille** | leaf |
| la **fleur** | flower |
| la :haie | hedge |
| l'herbe | grass |
| une ombre | shadow |
| la **pâquerette** | daisy |
| la **pierre** | stone, rock |
| la **plante** | plant |
| la **rose*** | rose |
| la **terre** | earth, ground |
| la **tulipe** | tulip |

les **feuilles** jaunissent et tombent des arbres the leaves turn yellow and fall off the trees

les **fleurs** poussent the flowers grow

cueillir un bouquet de **fleurs** to pick a bunch of flowers

**fleuri, en fleur(s)** in bloom; in blossom; in flower

tailler la **haie** to cut or trim the hedge

sous l'**ombre** d'un arbre in the shade of a tree

rester à l'**ombre** to remain in the shadows or in the shade

par **terre** on the ground

en l'air in(to) the air

**planter** to plant

**déplanter** to dig up; to transplant

## ** LE JARDIN ET LES FLEURS

| | |
|---|---|
| un **arrosoir** | watering can |
| le **banc** (de jardin) | (garden) seat |
| le **chrysanthème** | chrysanthemum |
| le **coquelicot** | poppy |
| le **crocus** | crocus |
| le **feuillage** | leaves |
| le **lierre** | ivy |
| le **lilas** | lilac |
| le **lis** [lis] | lily |
| le **muguet** | lily of the valley |
| un **œillet** | carnation |
| un **outil** | tool |
| le **pavillon**\* | summer house |
| le **pavot** | poppy |
| le **ver** | worm |

## *** LE JARDIN ET LES FLEURS

| | |
|---|---|
| un **arbuste** | shrub, bush |
| le **bassin** | (ornamental) pool |
| le **bourgeon** | bud |
| le **chèvrefeuille** | honeysuckle |
| l'**hortensia** | hydrangea |
| le **jardin potager** | vegetable garden |
| le **parterre**\* | border, flower bed |
| le **perce-neige** (pl inv) | snowdrop |
| le **pissenlit** | dandelion |
| le **pois de senteur** | sweet pea |
| le **potager** | kitchen or vegetable garden |
| le **sécateur** (à haie) | hedge-cutters |
| le **soleil**\*, le **tournesol** | sunflower |
| le **tuyau d'arrosage** | hose |

**arroser** les fleurs to water the flowers
**cultiver** des légumes to grow vegetables
**houer** le sol to hoe the ground
**ratisser** les feuilles to rake up the leaves
un **coin** ensoleillé/ombragé a sunny/shady spot
un **brin** de muguet a sprig of lily of the valley

## ** LE JARDIN ET LES FLEURS

| | |
|---|---|
| la brouette | wheelbarrow |
| la culture* | cultivation |
| une épine | thorn |
| les graines | seeds |
| la guêpe | wasp |
| la marguerite | daisy |
| les mauvaises herbes | weeds |
| la serre | greenhouse |
| la tondeuse | lawnmower |
| la violette | violet |

## *** LE JARDIN ET LES FLEURS

| | |
|---|---|
| une allée | path |
| la baie* | berry |
| la clôture | fence |
| la giroflée jaune | wallflower |
| la jacinthe | hyacinth |
| la jonquille | daffodil |
| une orchidée | orchid |
| la pelouse* | lawn |
| la pensée* | pansy |
| la plate-bande (pl. plates-bandes) | flower bed |
| la primevère | primrose |
| la racine | root |
| la renoncule | buttercup |
| la rocaille | rockery, rock garden |
| la rosée | dew |
| la semence | seed (in general) |
| la tige | stalk |

s'écorcher la main sur une épine to scratch one's hand on a thorn

semer les graines to sow the seed

la guêpe/l'abeille pique the wasp/bee stings

arracher les mauvaises herbes to pull out the weeds

désherber le jardin to weed the garden, do the weeding

## * LES LÉGUMES

| | |
|---|---|
| le chou *(pl -x)* | cabbage |
| le chou-fleur *(pl choux-fleurs)* | cauliflower |
| les épinards | spinach |
| le:haricot | bean |
| le:haricot vert | French bean |
| les légumes | vegetables |
| un oignon [ɔɲɔ̃] | onion |
| les petits pois | (garden) peas |
| le poireau *(pl -x)* | leek |

## ** LES LÉGUMES

| | |
|---|---|
| le champignon | mushroom |
| le chou *(pl -x)* de Bruxelles | Brussels sprout |
| le concombre | cucumber |
| le persil [pɛʀsi] | parsley |

## *** LES LÉGUMES

| | |
|---|---|
| l'ail [aj] | garlic |
| un artichaut | artichoke |
| le céleri | celery |
| le cresson | cress |
| un épi de maïs [ma-is] | corn on the cob |
| le navet | turnip |
| le piment doux, le poivron | (sweet) pepper |
| le radis | radish |

**cultiver des légumes** to grow vegetables
**occupe-toi de tes oignons!** mind your own business!
**la choucroute garni** sauerkraut with meat
**pommes persillées** potatoes sprinkled with parsley
**une tête/une gousse d'ail** a head/a clove of garlic
**saucisson à l'ail** garlic sausage

**\* LES LÉGUMES**

| | |
|---|---|
| la carotte | carrot |
| la pomme de terre (*pl* pommes de terre) | potato |
| la tomate | tomato; tomato plant |

**\*\* LES LÉGUMES**

| | |
|---|---|
| la laitue | lettuce |
| la salade (verte) | (green) salad |

**\*\*\* LES LÉGUMES**

| | |
|---|---|
| les asperges | asparagus |
| une aubergine | aubergine |
| la betterave | beetroot |
| la chicorée | endive |
| la courge | marrow |
| la courgette | courgette |
| une endive | chicory |

**carottes râpées** grated carrot
**pommes vapeur** boiled potatoes
**rouge comme une tomate** as red as a beetroot
**brasser** *or* **remuer** *or* **fatiguer la salade** to toss the salad

\* LA LOI

| | |
|---|---|
| un **agent** (de police) | policeman |
| un **agent secret** | secret agent |
| l'**argent**\* | silver; money |
| un **assassin** | murderer |
| le **barreau** (pl -x) | bar (of prison) |
| le **bulletin d'informations** | news bulletin |
| le **commissariat de police** | police station |
| le **courage** | bravery |
| le **crime** | crime |
| un **espion** | spy |
| le **fusil** [fyzi] | gun |
| le **gendarme** | gendarme |
| le **héros** | hero |
| un **hold-up** (pl inv) | hold-up |
| un **incendie** | fire |
| un **inspecteur de police** | police inspector |
| le **juge** | judge |
| le **meurtre** | murder |
| le **meurtrier** | murderer |
| l'**or** | gold |
| le **policier** | policeman |
| le **prisonnier** | prisoner |
| le **propriétaire** | owner |
| le **reportage** | report |
| le **révolutionnaire** | revolutionary |
| le **témoin** | witness |
| le **type** | fellow, chap |
| le **vol**\* | robbery |
| le **voleur** | robber, thief |

**commettre un crime** to commit a crime
**tirer sur** to shoot at; **assassiner** to murder; **tuer** to kill; **voler** to steal; to rob
**emprisonner** to imprison; **libérer** to set free
**ils l'ont fait prisonnier** they took him prisoner
**le signalement du voleur** the description of the robber
**un policier en civil** a plain-clothes policeman

**\* LA LOI**

| | |
|---|---|
| une accusation | charge; accusation |
| l'accusation | the prosecution |
| une arrestation | arrest |
| la bande\* | gang |
| la banque | bank |
| la carte d'identité | identity card |
| la défense | defence |
| la dispute | argument, dispute |
| une enquête | inquiry |
| la gendarmerie | headquarters of gendarmes |
| l'héroïne | heroine |
| la loi | law |
| la prise (de) | capture (of) |
| la prison | prison |
| la propriétaire | owner |
| la révolution | revolution |
| la tentative | attempt |

**arrêter/vaincre quelqu'un** to arrest/overpower somebody

**manifester** to hold a demonstration

**il a été condamné à 5 ans de prison** he got a 5 year prison sentence, he was sentenced to 5 years in prison

**dévaliser une banque** to rob a bank

## ** LA LOI

| | |
|---|---|
| le bandit | bandit |
| le cachot | dungeon, cell |
| le cambriolage | burglary |
| le cambrioleur | burglar, robber |
| le chef-d'œuvre (*pl* chefs-d'œuvre) | masterpiece |
| le chèque (de voyage) | (traveller's) cheque |
| le contrôle | control, check |
| le coup (de fusil) | (gun) shot |
| le criminel | criminal |
| le détournement | hijacking |
| un enlèvement | kidnapping |
| un ennemi | enemy |
| un escroc [ɛskro] | crook |
| le flic | 'cop' |
| le gangster | gangster |
| le garde | guard |
| le gardien de nuit | night watchman |
| le gouvernement | government |
| un inventaire | inventory |
| le lingot | ingot |
| le manifestant | demonstrator |
| le mort | dead man |
| un otage | hostage |
| le porte-feuille | wallet |
| le porte-monnaie | purse |
| le procès | trial |
| le radioreportage | radio report |
| le sauvetage | rescue |
| le sauveteur | rescuer |
| le voyou | hooligan |

**un cambriolage a eu lieu** a burglary has taken place
**prendre en otage** to take hostage
**être en otage** to be held hostage
**un vol à main armée, une attaque à main armée** an armed robbery, a hold-up
**une bande de voyous** a bunch of hooligans

## ** LA LOI

| | |
|---|---|
| une agglomération | built-up area |
| une amende | fine |
| une arme | weapon |
| une armée | army |
| la bagarre | fight, scuffle |
| la cellule | cell |
| la déposition | statement |
| une émeute | uprising |
| une évasion | escape |
| l'incarcération | imprisonment |
| la manifestation | demonstration |
| la mort | death |
| la morte | dead woman |
| la pancarte | placard |
| la peine de mort | death penalty |
| la preuve | proof |
| la rafle | raid |
| la rançon | ransom |

au secours! help!; à l'assassin! murder!
au voleur! stop thief!; au feu! fire!
haut les mains! hands up!
rendez-vous! give yourselves up!
sous peine d'amende on penalty of a fine
se battre (avec) to fight (with)
se bagarrer to fight, scuffle
le prisonnier s'est évadé de la prison the prisoner
  escaped from prison
en plein jour in broad daylight
faire sauter un bâtiment to blow up a building
sain et sauf safe and sound

### *** LA LOI

| | |
|---|---|
| le butin | loot |
| le cadavre | corpse |
| le détective privé | private detective |
| un évadé | escapee, escaped prisoner |
| le garde chargé de la sécurité | security guard |
| le juré | juryman |
| le jury | jury |
| le palais de justice | law courts |
| le pirate de l'air | hijacker |
| le revolver [REVƆLVER] | revolver |
| le terroriste | terrorist |

**interroger un témoin** to question a witness
**menacer quelqu'un** to threaten somebody
**un prisonnier (mis) en liberté provisoire** a prisoner on parole

***  LA LOI
| | |
|---|---|
| les drogues | drugs |
| une ordonnance* | decree, police order |
| la récompense | reward |

selon l'ordonnance de by the decree of
récompenser quelqu'un to reward somebody
graisser la patte à quelqu'un to bribe somebody

**\* LES LOISIRS**

| | |
|---|---|
| un **appareil** (photographique) | camera |
| l'**argent de poche** | pocket money |
| le **bal** | dance |
| le **billet** | ticket |
| le **camping\*** | camping; camp-site |
| le **chanteur** (pop) | (pop) singer |
| le **cinéma** | cinema |
| le **concert** | concert |
| le **concours\*** | competition |
| le **débutant** | beginner |
| le **disque** | record |
| un **électrophone** | record player |
| l'**enthousiasme** | enthusiasm |
| le **film** | film |
| le **guichet\*** | booking office |
| un **intérêt** | interest |
| le **jeu\*** (pl -x) | acting; game; gambling |
| le **juke-box** | jukebox |
| les **loisirs** | leisure activities; spare time |
| le **magnétophone** (à cassettes) | (cassette) recorder |
| les **mots croisés** | crossword puzzle |
| le **musée** | museum |
| un **orchestre\*** | orchestra |
| le **passe-temps** (pl inv) | hobby |
| le **pique-nique** (pl pique-niques) | picnic |
| le **programme** | (TV) programme |
| le **roman** | novel |
| le **spectacle** | show |
| le **théâtre** | theatre |
| le **transistor** | transistor |
| le **week-end** | weekend; at the weekend |

**faire du camping** to go camping
**aller au cinéma** to go to the cinema
**passer un disque** to put on a record
**s'intéresser à la musique pop/aux sports** to be interested in pop music/in sport

## * LES LOISIRS

| | |
|---|---|
| les actualités | news |
| la boîte de nuit | night club |
| la chaîne* | (TV) channel |
| la chanson | singing; song |
| la chanteuse (pop) | (pop) singer |
| la collection | collection; collecting |
| la colonie de vacances | holiday camp |
| la discothèque* | discotheque |
| une exposition | exhibition |
| la lecture | reading |
| la maison des jeunes | youth club |
| la musique pop/ classique | pop/classical music |
| la photo | photo |
| la photographie | photography; photograph |
| la promenade* | walk; trip, outing |
| la radio | radio |
| la réunion | meeting |
| la télévision, la télé | television, TV |
| la tente | tent |
| la vedette* (de cinéma) | (film) star |

prendre des photos (de) to take photos (of)

faire une promenade to go for a walk

faire une promenade en vélo/en voiture to go for a bike-ride/a drive

écouter la radio to listen to the radio

regarder la télévision to watch television

on se réunit tous les vendredis we meet every Friday

** LES LOISIRS

| | |
|---|---|
| le babyfoot | table football |
| le cercle dramatique | dramatic society |
| le club des jeunes | youth club |
| le club de photo | camera club |
| le correspondant | penfriend |
| un éclaireur | boy scout |
| l'ennui | boredom |
| le fan [fan] | fan |
| le roman-feuilleton | serial |
| le roman policier | thriller |
| le scout | boy scout |
| le tourne-disque (pl | |
| tourne-disques) | record player |

*** LES LOISIRS

| | |
|---|---|
| un appareil à sous | one-armed bandit, slot machine |
| le bricoleur | handyman, do-it-yourselfer |
| le bridge | bridge (game) |
| les échecs | chess |
| le flipper [flipœr] | pinball machine |
| le :hit-parade | hit parade |
| le microsillon | L.P., long-player |
| un opéra | opera |
| le palmarès | hit parade |
| le petit ami | boyfriend |
| le 45 tours | single (record) |
| le scoutisme | scouting |
| le tricot* | knitting |

**s'amuser/s'ennuyer (à faire quelque chose)** to enjoy oneself/to get bored (doing something)
**jouer aux cartes/aux échecs/aux dames** to play cards/chess/draughts
**faire collection de timbres** to collect stamps
**faire son tricot** to do one's knitting
**bricoler** to do odd jobs, potter about

## ** LES LOISIRS

| | |
|---|---|
| la bande* | (recording) tape |
| la bande dessinée | cartoon strip |
| la caméra | cine camera |
| les cartes* | cards |
| la correspondante | penfriend |
| la couture | sewing, dressmaking |
| une éclaireuse | girl guide |
| une émission | (TV) programme |
| la galerie d'art | art gallery |
| la peinture | painting; paint |
| la tapisserie* | tapestry |

## *** LES LOISIRS

| | |
|---|---|
| la boum | party |
| la chorale | choir |
| les dames | draughts |
| la diapositive | slide, transparency |
| une épreuve | (photographic) print |
| la pellicule | film (for camera) |
| la petite amie | girlfriend |
| la planche à roulettes | skateboard |
| la surprise-party (pl surprise-parties) | party |

passer son temps à faire quelque chose to spend one's time doing something
faire une partie de cartes to have a game of cards
faire partie de la chorale to sing in the choir
faire partie de l'orchestre to play in the orchestra

## * LES MAGASINS ET LES MARCHANDS

| | |
|---|---|
| l'argent* | money |
| un article | article |
| le boucher | butcher |
| le boulanger | baker |
| le bureau* (pl -x) | office |
| le bureau de poste | post office |
| le cadeau (pl -x) | present |
| le café* | café |
| le charcutier | pork butcher |
| le client* | customer, client |
| le comptoir | counter |
| le confiseur | confectioner |
| un employé* | employee; clerk |
| un épicier | grocer |
| le fruitier | fruiterer |
| le grand magasin | department store, general store |
| le magasin | shop |
| le marché* | deal; market |
| le prix* | price |
| le produit | product, produce |
| le restaurant | restaurant |
| au rez-de-chaussée | on ground level, on the ground floor |
| au sous-sol | in the basement |
| le supermarché | supermarket |
| le tabac* | tobacconist's |

acheter/vendre quelque chose to buy/sell something
quel est le prix de ce manteau? how much does this coat cost?
ça coûte combien? how much does that cost?
ça fait combien? how much is (all) that?
je l'ai payé 5 francs I paid 5 francs for it
chez le boucher/le boulanger at the butcher's/the baker's
faire des achats to do some shopping
faire son marché to do one's shopping
le marché aux puces the flea market

**\* LES MAGASINS ET LES MARCHANDS**

| | |
|---|---|
| l'addition | bill |
| une alimentation générale | general food store |
| la banque | bank |
| la bibliothèque* | library |
| la boucherie | butcher's (shop) |
| la boulangerie | baker's (shop) |
| la caisse* | till; cash desk |
| la charcuterie | pork butcher's |
| la cliente* | customer, client |
| les commissions | shopping |
| la compagnie | company |
| la confiserie | sweetshop, confectioner's |
| une course* | errand |
| les courses | shopping |
| une employée | employee |
| une épicerie | grocer's (shop) |
| la librairie | bookshop |
| la (petite) monnaie | (small) change |
| la pharmacie | chemist's (shop) |
| la poste* | post office |
| la queue* [kø] | queue |
| la vendeuse | shop assistant, salesgirl |
| la vitrine | shop window |

faire les commissions *or* les courses to go shopping
vendre des chemises/des choux-fleurs to sell shirts/cauliflowers
payez à la caisse pay at the cash desk
faire la queue to queue (up)
faire du lèche-vitrines to go window-shopping
mettre de l'argent à la banque to put money into the bank
retirer de l'argent à la banque to take money out of the bank

## ** LES MAGASINS ET LES MARCHANDS

| | |
|---|---|
| un acheteur | buyer |
| un agent immobilier | estate agent |
| le bijoutier | jeweller |
| le bon | form, coupon |
| le café-tabac | café (which sells tobacco etc) |
| le centre commercial | shopping centre |
| le chèque | cheque |
| le coiffeur | hairdresser; barber |
| le coloris | colour |
| le commerçant | tradesman |
| l'horloger | watchmaker |
| le magasin de chaussures | shoe shop |
| le mannequin* | dummy, model |
| le marchand de fruits | fruiterer |
| le marchand de journaux | newsagent |
| le marchand de légumes | greengrocer |
| le marchand de poisson, le poissonnier | fishmonger |
| le rayon* | department, counter |
| le tailleur* | tailor |

c'est trop cher it's too dear
c'est bon marché it's cheap
c'est meilleur marché it's cheaper
dépenser trop d'argent to spend too much money
garantir to guarantee
le bon de garantie guarantee form
le rayon alimentation/parfumerie the food/
perfume department or counter
c'est pour offrir? is it for a present? (i.e. would you
like it gift-wrapped?)

## ** LES MAGASINS ET LES MARCHANDS

| | |
|---|---|
| une agence immobilière | estate agency |
| la bijouterie | jeweller's (shop) |
| la boutique | small shop |
| la caisse d'épargne | savings bank |
| la compagnie d'assurances | insurance company |
| la droguerie | dispensing chemist's |
| une encolure | collar size |
| l'horlogerie | watchmaker's |
| la maison de commerce | firm |
| la maison de couture | fashion house |
| les marchandises | goods, wares |
| la parfumerie | perfumery counter or department |
| la pointure | shoe size |
| la société d'assurance | insurance company |
| la taille* | size |
| la vente | (action) sale; (technique) selling; (service) sales |

S.A. (société anonyme) Ltd.
'en vente ici' 'on sale here'
'maison à vendre' 'house for sale'
une voiture d'occasion a secondhand car

### *** LES MAGASINS ET LES MARCHANDS

| | |
|---|---|
| un agent de tourisme | travel agent |
| le bibliothécaire | librarian |
| le bookmaker | bookmaker |
| le cabinet de consultation | surgery |
| le commerce | trade, business |
| le cordonnier | cobbler |
| le débit de fritures | fish-and-chip shop |
| le débit de tabac | tobacconist's |
| le disquaire | record dealer |
| l'hypermarché | hypermarket |
| le libraire | bookseller |
| le marchand de biens | estate agent |
| le marchand de nouveautés | draper |
| le marchand des quatre saisons | barrow-boy, coster-monger |
| un opticien | optician |
| le pâtissier | confectioner, pastrycook |
| le pub | pub |
| le quincaillier | ironmonger |
| les soldes | sales; bargains |
| le zinc | counter (*of bar or pub*) |

**payer en espèces/par chèque** to pay cash/by cheque
**'en solde'** 'sale price', 'bargain'

### *** LES MAGASINS ET LES MARCHANDS

| | |
|---|---|
| une agence de voyages, une agence de tourisme | travel agency |
| la blanchisserie | laundry, dry cleaner's |
| la boutique d'animaux | pet shop |
| la crémerie | dairy |
| la devanture | shop window; display |
| la laiterie | dairy |
| la laverie automatique | launderette |
| la papeterie | stationer's |
| la pâtisserie | cake shop, confectioner's |
| la quincaillerie | ironmonger's, hardware shop |
| la saison des soldes | sales-time |
| la société de crédit immobilier | building society |
| la succursale | branch |

livrer les marchandises to deliver goods
étaler ses marchandises to display *or* spread out one's wares
à la devanture in the shop window; on display

\* LA MAISON—EN GÉNÉRAL

| | |
|---|---|
| un appartement | flat |
| le cabinet de toilette | toilet |
| le concierge | caretaker |
| le confort | comfort |
| le couloir | corridor |
| le décor* | decoration |
| un escalier | stairs, staircase |
| un étage | floor, storey |
| le garage | garage |
| le grand immeuble | block of flats |
| le grenier* | attic |
| le jardin | garden |
| le logement | housing; accommodation |
| les meubles | furniture |
| un meuble | a piece of furniture |
| le mur | wall |
| le plafond | ceiling |
| le plancher | floor |
| le propriétaire | owner; landlord |
| au rez-de-chaussée | on ground level, on the ground floor |
| le salon | lounge, living room |
| le sous-sol | basement |
| le toit | roof |
| le vestibule | hall |
| le voisin | neighbour |

**habiter un appartement/une maison jumelle** to live in a flat/a semi-detached
**la maison comprend 5 pièces** the house has 5 rooms
**meubler une pièce** to furnish a room
**monter/descendre (l'escalier)** to go upstairs/downstairs
**en bas** downstairs; **en haut** upstairs
**au premier/deuxième étage** on the first/second floor
**jusqu'au plafond** up to the ceiling
**au sous-sol** in the basement

## * LA MAISON—EN GÉNÉRAL

| | |
|---|---|
| la boue | mud |
| la cave | cellar |
| la chambre (à coucher) | bedroom |
| la cheminée* | chimney; fireplace; mantelpiece |
| la clef, la clé | key |
| la concierge | caretaker |
| la cuisine* | kitchen; cooking |
| l'entrée* | entrance (hall) |
| la famille | family |
| la femme de ménage | cleaning woman |
| la fenêtre | window |
| la fumée | smoke |
| la maison | house |
| la pièce* | room |
| la porte | door |
| la porte d'entrée | front door |
| la propriétaire | owner; landlady |
| la salle* | room |
| la salle de bains | bathroom |
| la salle à manger | dining room |
| la salle de séjour | living room |
| la voisine | neighbour |

à la maison at home
rentrer à la maison to go back home
chez moi/toi/nous/lui *etc* at my/your/our/his place
*etc*
un trousseau de clefs a bunch of keys
faire construire une maison to have a house built
faire la cuisine to do the cooking
entrer dans une salle to enter a room
regarder par la fenêtre to look out of the window

## ** LA MAISON—EN GÉNÉRAL

| | |
|---|---|
| le balcon* | balcony |
| le bâtiment | building |
| le cabinet de travail | study |
| le chauffage central | central heating |
| le déménagement | removal |
| le locataire | tenant |
| le loyer | rent |
| le parquet | (parquet or wooden) floor |
| le pavillon* | (small) house, detached house |
| le store | blind |
| le verrou | bolt |

## *** LA MAISON—EN GÉNÉRAL

| | |
|---|---|
| le bungalow | bungalow |
| le carreau (pl -x) | (floor) tile; (window) pane |
| le contrevent | shutter |
| le débarras | box room, junk room |
| le garde-manger | larder |
| le palier | landing |
| le plâtre* | plaster |
| le rebord de la fenêtre | window ledge, window sill |
| le seuil | doorstep |
| le studio | (one-roomed) flatlet |
| le tuyau (pl -x) d'écoulement or d'évacuation | drainpipe |
| le volet | shutter |

déménager dans une autre ville to move (house) to
  another town
emménager to move in
s'installer to settle down, settle in
fermer les volets to close the shutters

**\*\* LA MAISON—EN GÉNÉRAL**

| | |
|---|---|
| une antenne | aerial |
| la chambre d'ami | spare room |
| la locataire | tenant |
| la loge* | caretaker's room |
| la maison jumelle | semi-detached house |
| la marche | step |
| la ménagère | housewife |
| la porte-fenêtre (pl portes-fenêtres), | |
| la porte vitrée | French window |
| la sonnette | (door)bell |
| la villa | (detached) house |
| la vitre | (window) pane |

**\*\*\* LA MAISON—EN GÉNÉRAL**

| | |
|---|---|
| une ardoise | slate |
| la chaudière | boiler |
| la chaumière | (thatched) cottage |
| la façade | front (of house) |
| la gouttière | gutter |
| la lucarne | skylight |
| la mansarde | attic |
| la paroi | partition |
| la serrure | lock |
| la tuile | (roof) tile |

on a sonné the doorbell rang, somebody rang
frapper à la porte to knock at the door

* LA MAISON—EN PARTICULIER

| | |
|---|---|
| un aspirateur | vacuum cleaner, hoover |
| le bain* | bath |
| le chiffon | duster; rag |
| le couvercle | lid |
| le dentifrice | toothpaste |
| le déodorant | deodorant |
| un électrophone | record player |
| le fer (à repasser) | iron |
| le feu (pl -x) | fire |
| le frigidaire, le frigo | fridge |
| le gaz | gas |
| le lavabo | washbasin |
| le ménage | housework |
| le miroir | mirror |
| le placard | cupboard |
| le plateau* (pl -x) | tray |
| le poste de télévision | television set |
| le réveil, le réveille-matin | alarm clock |
| le savon | soap |
| le téléviseur | television |
| le torchon* | dishcloth |

prendre un bain, se baigner to take a bath

à feu doux on a low heat

faire le ménage to do the housework

se regarder dans le miroir to look at oneself in
  the mirror

brancher/débrancher un appareil (électrique) to
  plug in/to unplug an (electrical) appliance

## * LA MAISON—EN PARTICULIER

| | |
|---|---|
| les affaires* | things |
| une armoire | wardrobe |
| la baignoire | bath |
| la boîte aux lettres* | letterbox |
| la brosse | brush |
| la brosse à dents | toothbrush |
| la casserole | pan, saucepan |
| la douche | shower |
| l'eau | water |
| une échelle | ladder |
| l'électricité | electricity |
| la femme de ménage | cleaning woman |
| la glace* | mirror |
| la lessive | soap powder; washing |
| la lumière | light |
| les ordures | rubbish, refuse |
| la poignée* | handle |
| la recette | recipe |
| la serviette* | towel |
| la télévision | television |
| la vaisselle | dishes |

ranger ses affaires to tidy up one's things

laisser traîner ses affaires partout to leave one's
things lying about everywhere

faire cuire quelque chose dans une casserole to
cook something in a pan

faire frire to fry; faire bouillir to boil; faire griller
to grill

l'eau coule dans l'évier the water flows into the sink

faire la lessive to do the washing

faire la vaisselle to wash the dishes, do the washing-
up

faire le repassage to do the ironing

à la télévision on television

allumer/éteindre la télé to switch on/off the TV

ouvrir/fermer la lumière to switch on/off the light

** LA MAISON—EN PARTICULIER

| | |
|---|---|
| le balai | brush, broom |
| le coussin | cushion |
| le moulin à café | coffee grinder |
| le nettoyage | cleaning |
| le séchoir à cheveux | hair-drier |
| le shampooing [ʃãpwɛ̃] | shampoo |
| le vase | vase |

*** LA MAISON—EN PARTICULIER

| | |
|---|---|
| le balai mécanique | carpet sweeper |
| le bibelot | ornament |
| le blaireau (pl -x) | shaving brush |
| le cendrier | ashtray |
| le cintre | coat hanger |
| le drap* | sheet |
| un édredon | quilt, eiderdown |
| un essuie-mains (pl inv) | hand towel |
| un évier | sink |
| le grille-pain | toaster |
| un interrupteur | switch |
| le mixeur | (electric) mixer |
| un oreiller | pillow |
| le paillasson | doormat |
| le papier peint | wallpaper |
| le rasoir | razor |
| le robinet | tap |
| le seau (pl -x) | bucket |
| le seau (pl -x) à charbon | coal scuttle |
| le tisonnier | poker |
| le traversin | bolster |
| le tuyau (pl -x) | pipe |

**balayer** to sweep
**nettoyer** to clean
**épousseter** to dust
**passer l'aspirateur** to vacuum, hoover
**le (grand) nettoyage de printemps** the spring-cleaning

## ** LA MAISON—EN PARTICULIER

| | |
|---|---|
| la corbeille* (à papier) | waste paper basket |
| la discothèque* | record cabinet, record rack |
| la marmite | pot |
| la peinture* | paint; painting |
| la poêle [pwal] | frying pan |
| la poussière | dust |
| la tapisserie* | wallpaper |

## *** LA MAISON—EN PARTICULIER

| | |
|---|---|
| la balance | weighing scales |
| la boîte à ordures | dustbin |
| la bouilloire | kettle |
| la bouillotte | hot water bottle |
| la cocotte-minute | pressure cooker |
| la couette | continental quilt, duvet |
| la couverture | rug; blanket; cover |
| la couverture chauffante | electric blanket |
| la cruche | jug |
| la descente de lit | bedside rug |
| une éponge | sponge |
| une essoreuse | spin dryer |
| la lame | blade |
| la moquette | fitted carpet |
| la planche à repasser | ironing board |
| la poubelle | dustbin |

jeter quelque chose à la poubelle to throw something in the dustbin

**\* LES MATÉRIAUX**

| | |
|---|---|
| l'argent* | silver |
| le bois | wood |
| le caoutchouc | |
| [kautʃu] | rubber |
| le coton | cotton |
| le cuir | leather |
| le fil | thread |
| le fil de fer | wire |
| le gaz | gas |
| le métal (*pl* métaux) | metal |
| le nylon | nylon |
| l'or | gold |
| le papier | paper |
| le plastique | plastic |
| le satin | satin |
| le tissu | cloth, material |
| le velours | velvet |
| le verre | glass |

**\*\* LES MATÉRIAUX**

| | |
|---|---|
| l'acier | steel |
| le bronze | bronze |
| le charbon | coal |
| le cristal | crystal |
| le fer | iron |
| le velours côtelé | cord, corduroy |

une chaise *etc* de *or* en bois a wooden chair *etc*
les bottes (*fpl*) de caoutchouc wellington boots
j'ai les bras/les jambes en coton my arms/my legs
  feel like jelly *or* like cotton wool
le papier d'étain tinfoil, silver paper
le papier hygiénique toilet paper
le fer forgé wrought iron

## * LES MATÉRIAUX

| | |
|---|---|
| l'essence | petrol |
| la ficelle | string |
| la fourrure | fur |
| l'huile | oil |
| la laine | wool |
| la pierre | stone |
| la soie | silk |

## ** LES MATÉRIAUX

| | |
|---|---|
| la brique | brick |
| la corde* | rope |
| la dentelle | lace |
| la faïence | earthenware, pottery |
| la paille | straw |
| la peau de mouton | sheepskin |
| la peau de porc | pigskin |
| la porcelaine | porcelain, china |
| la toile | linen; canvas |

un bout de ficelle a piece of string
un manteau en fourrure a fur coat
une pierre précieuse a precious stone, a gem
la corde raide the tightrope
la corde à sauter the skipping rope
un chapeau de paille a straw hat
des gants en peau de mouton sheepskin gloves
une canadienne a sheepskin jacket

*** LES MATÉRIAUX

| | |
|---|---|
| l'acrylique | acrylic (fibre) |
| le béton | concrete |
| le caoutchouc mousse | foam rubber |
| le carton | cardboard |
| le ciment | cement |
| le cuivre | copper |
| le cuivre jaune | brass |
| le daim | suede |
| le drap* | woollen cloth |
| l'étain | tin; pewter |
| le fer-blanc | tin, tinplate |
| le granit | granite |
| le jean* [dʒin] | denim |
| le lin | flax |
| le liquide | liquid |
| le marbre | marble |
| les matériaux | materials |
| l'osier | wickerwork |
| le pétrole | oil, petroleum; paraffin |
| le plâtre* | plaster |
| le plomb | lead |
| le suède | suede |
| le tergal | terylene |
| le tweed | tweed |
| le vinyle | vinyl |

une boîte en carton, un carton a cardboard box

*** LES MATÉRIAUX

| | |
|---|---|
| l'argile | clay |
| la cire | wax |
| la colle* | glue |
| la cotonnade | cotton fabric |
| l'étoffe | material |
| la:houille | (industrial) coal |

la houille blanche hydroelectric power

**\* LES MEUBLES**

| | |
|---|---|
| un électrophone | record player |
| le fauteuil | armchair |
| le feu *(pl -x)* | fire |
| le lit | bed |
| les meubles | furniture |
| un meuble | a piece of furniture |
| le placard | cupboard |
| le rayon\* | shelf |
| le rideau *(pl -x)* | curtain |
| le tableau *(pl -x)* | picture |
| le tapis | carpet, rug |
| le téléphone | telephone |
| le téléviseur (couleur) | (colour) television |
| le tiroir | drawer |

**meubler une pièce** to furnish a room
**un appartement meublé** a furnished flat
**un fauteuil à bascule** a rocking chair
**mettre le feu à quelque chose** to set fire to something, set something on fire
**allumer le feu** to light the fire
**prendre feu** to catch fire
**au feu!** fire!
**un feu d'artifice** a firework; a firework display
**un feu de joie** a bonfire
**faire le lit** to make the bed
**aller au lit** to go to bed
**il est au lit** he is in bed
**sauter à bas du lit** to jump out of bed
**tirer les rideaux** to draw the curtains
**au téléphone** on the telephone
**un coup de téléphone** a telephone call

**\* LES MEUBLES**

| | |
|---|---|
| une armoire | wardrobe |
| la baignoire | bath |
| la chaise | chair |
| la lampe (électrique) | lamp |
| la maison | house |
| la pièce\* | room |
| la radio | radio |
| la table | table |

une chaise de bébé a highchair
une chaise longue a deckchair; a chaise longue
une lampe de poche a torch
un appartement de 4 pièces a 4-roomed flat
mettre la table to lay or set the table
être à table to be having a meal
se mettre à table to sit down to eat, sit down at
  the table
à table! come and eat!, dinner (or lunch etc) is
  ready!
à la télévision on television
à la radio on the radio

## ** LES MEUBLES

| | |
|---|---|
| le buffet* | sideboard |
| le bureau* (pl -x) | bureau, writing desk |
| le canapé | settee, couch |
| le coffre* | chest |
| le four | oven |
| le lit d'enfant | cot |
| le matelas | mattress |
| le miroir | mirror |
| le piano | piano |
| le secrétaire* | writing desk |
| le store | blind |
| le tabouret | stool |
| le tourne-disque | |
| (pl tourne-disques) | record player |
| le transistor | transistor (radio) |

au four in the oven
un store vénitien a Venetian blind

## ** LES MEUBLES

| | |
|---|---|
| la bibliothèque* | bookcase |
| la coiffeuse* | dressing table |
| la commode | chest of drawers |
| la cuisinière* | |
| (électrique/à gaz) | (electric/gas) cooker |
| la glace* | mirror |
| la machine à laver | washing machine |
| la machine à laver | |
| la vaisselle | dishwashing machine, dishwasher |
| la peinture* | painting |
| la pendule | clock |
| la table de toilette | dressing table |

**une machine à coudre/à tricoter** a sewing/knitting machine

**une machine à écrire** a typewriter

**une pendule à coucou** a cuckoo clock

**une table à repasser** an ironing board *or* table

*** LES MEUBLES

| | |
|---|---|
| le **berceau** (*pl* -x) | cradle |
| le **cadre*** | frame |
| le **camion de** **déménagement** | removal van |
| le **congélateur** | freezer |
| le **déménagement** | removal |
| le **déménageur** | removal man |
| le **lampadaire** | standard lamp |
| le **mobilier** | furniture |
| le **porte-parapluies** | umbrella stand |
| le **radiateur à** **accumulation** | storage heater |

### *** LES MEUBLES

| | |
|---|---|
| une **applique** | wall light, wall lamp |
| la **chaîne stéréo** | stereo unit |
| une **étagère** | (set of) shelves |
| la **moquette** | fitted carpet |
| la **table basse** | coffee table |
| la **table de chevet** | bedside table |
| la **table roulante** | trolley |

\* LE MONDE

| | |
|---|---|
| le **chef-lieu** | chief town, county town |
| le **désert** | desert |
| un **étranger**\* | foreigner; stranger |
| à l'**étranger** | abroad |
| le **monde** | world |
| le **pays**\* | country |
| le **nord**: au **nord** | north: in *or* to the north |
| le **sud**: au **sud** | south: in *or* to the south |
| l'**est** (*m*): à l'**est** | east: in *or* to the east |
| l'**ouest** (*m*): | |
| à l'**ouest** | west: in *or* to the west |

\*\* LE MONDE

| | |
|---|---|
| le **canal** (*pl* canaux) | canal |
| le **continent** | continent |
| le **fleuve** | river |
| le **massif** | mountain range |
| un **océan** | ocean |
| le **plateau**\* (*pl* -x) | plateau |
| le **sommet** | summit |
| l'**univers** | universe |

\*\*\* LE MONDE

| | |
|---|---|
| l'**équateur** | equator |
| le **globe** | globe |
| le **peuple** | people, nation |
| le **pic**\* | mountain peak |
| le **tremblement de terre** | earthquake |
| les **tropiques** | tropics |
| le **volcan** | volcano |

faire le **tour** du **monde** to go round the world
le **meilleur** (la **meilleure**) du **monde** the best in the
  world
il y a beaucoup de **monde** there are lots of people
des **pays lointains** far-off countries
de quel **pays** venez-vous? what country do you come
  from?

**\* LE MONDE**

| | |
|---|---|
| la capitale | capital (city) |
| la carte\* | map |
| la colline | hill |
| la côte\* | coast |
| une étoile | star |
| une étrangère\* | foreigner; stranger |
| la forêt | forest |
| la lune | moon |
| la mer | sea |
| la montagne | mountain |
| la nation | nation, people |
| la nationalité | nationality |
| la planète | planet |
| la population | population |
| la région | region, area |
| la terre | earth |

**\*\* LE MONDE**

| | |
|---|---|
| la chaîne de montagnes | mountain range or chain |
| la frontière | border, frontier |
| une île | island |
| la plaine | plain |
| la province | province(s) |
| la vallée | valley |
| la zone | zone |

**\*\*\* LE MONDE**

| | |
|---|---|
| la mappemonde | map of the world; globe |
| la patrie | native country |
| la presqu'île | peninsula |
| la race | race |

passer l'hiver à la montagne/à la campagne/en ville
to spend the winter in the mountains/in the
country/in the town
ville frontière frontier or border town
de province provincial

**\* LES NATIONALITÉS**

| | |
|---|---|
| un **Allemand** | a German |
| un **Américain** | an American |
| un **Anglais** | an Englishman |
| un **Belge** | a Belgian |
| un **Espagnol** | a Spaniard |
| un **Français** | a Frenchman |
| un **Italien** | an Italian |
| un **Portugais** | a Portuguese |
| un **Suisse** | a Swiss |

**\*\* LES NATIONALITÉS**

| | |
|---|---|
| un **Africain** | an African |
| un **Arabe** | an Arab |
| un **Asiatique** | an Asian |
| un **Australien** | an Australian |
| un **Britannique** | a Briton |
| un **Canadien** | a Canadian |
| un **Chinois** | a Chinese |
| un **Écossais** | a Scotsman |
| un **Esquimau** | an Eskimo |
| un **Gallois** | a Welshman |
| un **:Hollandais** | a Dutchman |
| un **Indien** | an Indian |
| un **Irlandais** | an Irishman |
| un **Japonais** | a Japanese |
| un **Juif** | a Jew |
| un **Pakistanais** | a Pakistani |
| un **Peau-Rouge** | |
| (*pl* **Peaux-Rouges**) | a Red Indian |
| | |
| un **Canadien français** | a French Canadian |

## * LES NATIONALITÉS

| | |
|---|---|
| une **Allemande** | a German (girl or woman) |
| une **Américaine** | an American (girl or woman) |
| une **Anglaise** | an Englishwoman, an English girl |
| une **Belge** | a Belgian (girl or woman) |
| une **Espagnole** | a Spaniard, a Spanish girl or woman |
| une **Française** | a Frenchwoman, a French girl or woman |
| une **Italienne** | an Italian (girl or woman) |
| une **Portugaise** | a Portuguese (girl or woman) |
| une **Suisse** | a Swiss (girl or woman) |

## ** LES NATIONALITÉS

| | |
|---|---|
| une **Africaine** | an African (girl or woman) |
| une **Arabe** | an Arab (girl or woman) |
| une **Australienne** | an Australian (girl or woman) |
| une **Britannique** | a Briton, a British girl or woman |
| une **Canadienne** | a Canadian (girl or woman) |
| une **Chinoise** | a Chinese (girl or woman) |
| une **Écossaise** | a Scotswoman, a Scots girl |
| une **Esquimaude** | an Eskimo (girl or woman) |
| une **Galloise** | a Welshwoman, a Welsh girl |
| une **Hollandaise** | a Dutchwoman, a Dutch girl |
| une **Indienne** | an Indian (girl or woman) |
| une **Irlandaise** | an Irishwoman, an Irish girl |
| une **Japonaise** | a Japanese (girl or woman) |
| une **Juive** | a Jewish girl or woman |
| une **Pakistanaise** | a Pakistani (girl or woman) |

## \*\*\* LES NATIONALITÉS

| | |
|---|---|
| un **Algérien** | an Algerian |
| un **Autrichien** | an Austrian |
| un **Brésilien** | a Brazilian |
| un **Danois** | a Dane |
| un **Européen** | a European |
| un **Finnois**, un **Finlandais** | a Finn |
| un **Grec** | a Greek |
| un **Marocain** | a Moroccan |
| un **Mexicain** | a Mexican |
| un **Néo-Zélandais** | a New-Zealander |
| un **Norvégien** | a Norwegian |
| un **Polonais** | a Pole |
| un **Russe** | a Russian |
| un **Scandinave** | a Scandinavian |
| un **Suédois** | a Swede |
| un **Tchèque** | a Czech |
| un **Tunisien** | a Tunisian |
| un **Turc** | a Turk |
| un **Vietnamien** | a Vietnamese |
| un **Yougoslave** | a Yugoslav |

The forms given here and on the two preceding pages are the noun forms (i.e. for *people*) and begin with a capital letter:
il est **Danois** he is a Dane
elle est **Danoise** she is a Danish girl *etc.*

They can be used adjectivally by converting the capital into a small letter:
le paysage **danois** the Danish countryside
une ville **danoise** a Danish town

*** LES NATIONALITÉS

| | |
|---|---|
| une Algérienne | an Algerian (girl or woman) |
| une Autrichienne | an Austrian (girl or woman) |
| une Brésilienne | a Brazilian (girl or woman) |
| une Danoise | a Dane, a Danish girl or woman |
| une Finnoise, une Finlandaise | a Finn, a Finnish girl or woman |
| une Grecque | a Greek, a Greek girl or woman |
| une Marocaine | a Moroccan (girl or woman) |
| une Mexicaine | a Mexican (girl or woman) |
| une Néo-Zélandaise | a New-Zealander, a New Zealand girl or woman |
| une Norvégienne | a Norwegian (girl or woman) |
| une Polonaise | a Pole, a Polish girl or woman |
| une Russe | a Russian (girl or woman) |
| une Scandinave | a Scandinavian (girl or woman) |
| une Suédoise | a Swede, a Swedish girl or woman |
| une Tchèque | a Czech (girl or woman) |
| une Tunisienne | a Tunisian (girl or woman) |
| une Turque | a Turkish girl or woman |
| une Vietnamienne | a Vietnamese (girl or woman) |
| une Yougoslave | a Yugoslav, a Yugoslavian girl or woman |

## 1 Les nombres cardinaux   Cardinal numbers

| | | |
|---|---|---|
| nought | 0 | zéro |
| one | 1 | (m) un, (f) une |
| two | 2 | deux |
| three | 3 | trois |
| four | 4 | quatre |
| five | 5 | cinq |
| six | 6 | six |
| seven | 7 | sept |
| eight | 8 | huit |
| nine | 9 | neuf |
| ten | 10 | dix |
| eleven | 11 | onze |
| twelve | 12 | douze |
| thirteen | 13 | treize |
| fourteen | 14 | quatorze |
| fifteen | 15 | quinze |
| sixteen | 16 | seize |
| seventeen | 17 | dix-sept |
| eighteen | 18 | dix-huit |
| nineteen | 19 | dix-neuf |
| twenty | 20 | vingt |
| twenty-one | 21 | vingt et un |
| twenty-two | 22 | vingt-deux |
| twenty-three | 23 | vingt-trois |
| thirty | 30 | trente |
| thirty-one | 31 | trente et un |
| thirty-two | 32 | trente-deux |
| forty | 40 | quarante |
| fifty | 50 | cinquante |
| sixty | 60 | soixante |
| seventy | 70 | soixante-dix |
| seventy-one | 71 | soixante-et-onze |
| eighty | 80 | quatre-vingts |
| eighty-one | 81 | quatre-vingt-un |
| ninety | 90 | quatre-vingt-dix |
| ninety-one | 91 | quatre-vingt-onze |
| a (or one) hundred | 100 | cent |

## Les nombres cardinaux (*suite*)

| | | |
|---|---|---|
| a hundred and one | 101 | cent un |
| a hundred and two | 102 | cent deux |
| a hundred and ten | 110 | cent dix |
| a hundred and eighty-two | 182 | cent quatre-vingt-deux |
| two hundred | 200 | deux cents |
| two hundred and one | 201 | deux cent un |
| two hundred and two | 202 | deux cent deux |
| three hundred | 300 | trois cents |
| four hundred | 400 | quatre cents |
| five hundred | 500 | cinq cents |
| six hundred | 600 | six cents |
| seven hundred | 700 | sept cents |
| eight hundred | 800 | huit cents |
| nine hundred | 900 | neuf cents |
| a (or one) thousand | 1000 | mille |
| a thousand and one | 1001 | mille un |
| a thousand and two | 1002 | mille deux |
| two thousand | 2000 | deux mille |
| ten thousand | 10000 | dix mille |
| a (or one) hundred thousand | 100000 | cent mille |
| a (or one) million | 1000000 | un million |
| two million | 2000000 | deux millions |

**N.B.** 1000000: In French, the word *million* is a noun, so the numeral takes *de* when there is a following noun: *un million de gens, trois millions de maisons*

## 2 Les nombres ordinaux    Ordinal numbers

| | | |
|---|---|---|
| first | 1 | (m) premier, (f) -ière |
| second | 2 | deuxième |
| third | 3 | troisième |
| fourth | 4 | quatrième |
| fifth | 5 | cinquième |
| sixth | 6 | sixième |
| seventh | 7 | septième |
| eighth | 8 | huitième |
| ninth | 9 | neuvième |
| tenth | 10 | dixième |
| eleventh | 11 | onzième |
| twelfth | 12 | douzième |
| thirteenth | 13 | treizième |
| fourteenth | 14 | quatorzième |
| fifteenth | 15 | quinzième |
| sixteenth | 16 | seizième |
| seventeenth | 17 | dix-septième |
| eighteenth | 18 | dix-huitième |
| nineteenth | 19 | dix-neuvième |
| twentieth | 20 | vingtième |
| twenty-first | 21 | vingt et unième |
| twenty-second | 22 | vingt-deuxième |
| thirtieth | 30 | trentième |
| thirty-first | 31 | trente et unième |
| fortieth | 40 | quarantième |
| fiftieth | 50 | cinquantième |
| sixtieth | 60 | soixantième |
| seventieth | 70 | soixante-dixième |
| eightieth | 80 | quatre-vingtième |
| ninetieth | 90 | quatre-vingt-dixième |
| hundredth | 100 | centième |

## Les nombres ordinaux (suite)

| | | |
|---|---|---|
| hundred and first | 101 | cent unième |
| hundred and tenth | 110 | cent-dixième |
| two hundredth | 200 | deux centième |
| three hundredth | 300 | trois centième |
| four hundredth | 400 | quatre centième |
| five hundredth | 500 | cinq centième |
| six hundredth | 600 | six centième |
| seven hundredth | 700 | sept centième |
| eight hundredth | 800 | huit centième |
| nine hundredth | 900 | neuf centième |
| thousandth | 1000 | millième |
| two thousandth | 2000 | deux millième |
| millionth | 1000000 | millionième |
| two millionth | 2000000 | deux millionième |

## 3 Les fractions — Fractions

| | | |
|---|---|---|
| a half | $\frac{1}{2}$ | (m) un demi, (f) une demie |
| one and a half helpings | $1\frac{1}{2}$ | une portion et demie |
| two and a half kilos | $2\frac{1}{2}$ | deux kilos et demi |
| a third | $\frac{1}{3}$ | un tiers |
| two thirds | $\frac{2}{3}$ | deux tiers |
| a quarter | $\frac{1}{4}$ | un quart |
| three quarters | $\frac{3}{4}$ | trois quarts |
| a sixth | $\frac{1}{6}$ | un sixième |
| five and five sixths | $5\frac{5}{6}$ | cinq et cinq sixièmes |
| a twelfth | $\frac{1}{12}$ | un douzième |
| seven twelfths | $\frac{7}{12}$ | sept douzièmes |
| a hundredth | $\frac{1}{100}$ | un centième |
| a thousandth | $\frac{1}{1000}$ | un millième |

**une assiette de** a plate of
**une bande de** a group *or* gang of; a flock of (*birds*)
**beaucoup de (monde)** lots of (people)
**une boîte de** a tin *or* can of; a box of
**un bol de** a bowl of
**une bouchée de** a mouthful of
**un bout de papier** a bit *or* piece of paper
**une bouteille de** a bottle of
**cent grammes (mpl) de** a hundred grammes of
**une centaine de** (about) a hundred
**une cuillerée de** a spoonful of
**un demi de bière** half a litre of beer, 'a half'
**une demi-douzaine de** half a dozen
**un demi-kilo de** half a kilo of
**un demi-litre de** half a litre of
**une dizaine de** (about) ten
**une douzaine de** a dozen
**une foule de** a crowd of, crowds of, heaps of
**un kilo(gramme) de** a kilo(gramme) of
**un litre de** a litre of
**une livre de** a pound of
**un mètre de** a metre of
**des milliers de** thousands of
**un morceau de sucre** a lump of sugar
**un morceau de gâteau** a piece *or* slice of cake
**un paquet de** a packet of
**un peu de** a little, a trifle
**une pile de** a pile of
**la plupart de** *or* **des** most (of)
**une poignée\* de** a handful of
**une portion de** a portion *or* helping of
**un pot de** a pot *or* tub of; a jar of
**(une) quantité de** a lot of, many
**une tablette de** a bar of (*chocolate*)
**un tas de** a heap of, heaps of
**une tasse de** a cup(ful) of
**un tonneau de** a barrel of
**une tranche de** a slice of
**un troupeau de** a herd of (*cattle*); a flock of (*sheep*)
**un verre de** a glass of

## LES NOMS GÉOGRAPHIQUES (A)

| | |
|---|---|
| **Alger** | Algiers |
| **les Alpes** (*fpl*) | the Alps |
| **Anvers** | Antwerp |
| **Athènes** | Athens |
| **l'Atlantique** (*m*) | the Atlantic |
| **Bâle** | Basle |
| **Barcelone** | Barcelona |
| **Berlin** | Berlin |
| **Bruxelles** | Brussels |
| **Le Caire** | Cairo |
| **Cordoue** | Cordoba |
| **Corse** (*f*) | Corsica |
| **Douvres** | Dover |
| **Édimbourg** | Edinburgh |
| **l'Extrême-Orient** (*m*) | the Far East |
| **Gand** | Ghent |
| **Gênes** | Genoa |
| **Genève** | Geneva |
| **la Haye** | The Hague |
| **les îles Britanniques** | the British Isles |
| **les îles anglo-normandes** | the Channel Islands |
| **le Jura** | the Jura mountains |
| **le lac Léman** | Lake Geneva |
| **Lisbonne** | Lisbon |
| **la Loire** | the Loire |
| **Londres** | London |
| **Lyon** | Lyons |
| **Majorque** (*f*) | Majorca |
| **la Manche** | the English Channel |
| **Marseille** | Marseilles |
| **la (mer) Méditerranée** | the Mediterranean |
| **la mer du Nord** | the North Sea |
| **le Midi** | the Midi, the South of France |
| **Moscou** | Moscow |
| **le Moyen-Orient** | the Middle East |
| **le Pacifique** | the Pacific |
| **Paris** | Paris |
| **le Pôle nord/sud** | the North/South Pole |

## LES NOMS GÉOGRAPHIQUES (A) *(suite)*

| | |
|---|---|
| le Proche-Orient | the Near East |
| les Pyrénées *(fpl)* | the Pyrenees |
| Québec | Quebec *(city)* |
| le Québec | Quebec *(state)* |
| le Rhin | the Rhine |
| le Rhône | the Rhone |
| Sardaigne *(f)* | Sardinia |
| la Seine | the Seine |
| Sicile *(f)* | Sicily |
| la Tamise | the Thames |
| la Terre Sainte | the Holy Land |
| Varsovie | Warsaw |
| Venise | Venice |
| Vienne *(Autriche)* | Vienna |
| la Volga | the Volga |
| les Vosges *(fpl)* | the Vosges Mountains |

## LES NOMS GÉOGRAPHIQUES (B)

**arlésien, -ienne** of *or* from Arles
**bâlois, -oise** of *or* from Basle
**bavarois, -oise** of *or* from Bavaria, Bavarian
**bordelais, -aise** of *or* from Bordeaux
**bourguignon, -onne** of *or* from Burgundy, Burgundian
**breton, -onne** of *or* from Brittany, Breton
**bruxellois, -oise** of *or* from Brussels
**champenois, -oise** of *or* from Champagne
**corse** of *or* from Corsica, Corsican
**gascon, -onne** of *or* from Gascony, Gascon
**gaulois, -oise** of *or* from Gaul, Gallic
**genevois, -oise** of *or* from Geneva, Genevan
**liégeois, -oise** of *or* from Liège
**londonien, -ienne** of *or* from London
**lyonnais, -aise** of *or* from Lyons
**madrilène** of *or* from Madrid
**malouin, -ine** of *or* from Saint-Malo
**mannois, -oise** of *or* from the Isle of Man, Manx
**monégasque** of *or* from Monaco, Monacan
**montréalais, -aise** of *or* from Montreal

LES NOMS GÉOGRAPHIQUES (B) *(suite)*
**moscovite** of *or* from Moscow, Muscovite
**nancéien, -ienne** of *or* from Nancy
**nantais, -aise** of *or* from Nantes
**napolitain, -aine** of *or* from Naples, Neapolitan
**new-yorkais, -aise** of *or* from New York
**niçois, -oise** of *or* from Nice
**nîmois, -oise** of *or* from Nîmes
**normand, -ande** of *or* from Normandy, Norman
**oxonien, -ienne** of *or* from Oxford, Oxonian
**parisien, -ienne** of *or* from Paris, Parisian
**provençal, -ale** of *or* from Provence, Provençal
**pyrénéen, -enne** of *or* from the Pyrenees, Pyrenean
**québécois, -oise** of *or* from Quebec
**rémois, -oise** of *or* from Reims
**rouennais, -aise** of *or* from Rouen
**savoyard, -arde** of *or* from Savoy
**stéphanois, -oise** of *or* from St.-Étienne
**strasbourgeois, -oise** of *or* from Strasbourg
**tourangeau, -elle** of *or* from Touraine *or* Tours
**vénitien, -ienne** of *or* from Venice, Venetian
**vichyssois, -oise** of *or* from Vichy
**viennois, -oise** of *or* from Vienna *(Austria)*,
   Viennese; *or* Vienne *(France)*
**vosgien, -ienne** of *or* from the Vosges (Mountains)

The forms given above, beginning with small letters,
are the adjective forms:
**les boulevards parisiens**
**la région parisienne**
They can be converted into nouns by changing the
small letter to a capital:
**les Parisiens et les Parisiennes**

**\* LA NOURRITURE ET LES REPAS**

| | |
|---|---|
| le beurre | butter |
| le biscuit | biscuit |
| le bœuf\* | beef |
| le bol | bowl |
| le café\* | coffee |
| le chocolat | chocolate |
| le couteau (*pl* -x) | knife |
| le couvert | place setting |
| le croissant | croissant |
| le déjeuner | lunch |
| le dessert | dessert |
| le dîner | dinner |
| le fromage | cheese |
| les fruits | fruit |
| un fruit | a piece of fruit, some fruit |
| le gâteau (*pl* -x) | cake |
| le goûter | tea (*meal*) |
| les:hors-d'œuvre | hors d'œuvres, starters |
| le jambon | ham |
| le jus de fruit | fruit juice |
| le lait | milk |
| les légumes | vegetables |
| un œuf [œf] (*pl* -s [ø]) | egg |
| le pain | bread; loaf |
| le pâté\* | pâté |
| le petit déjeuner | breakfast |
| le plat | dish; course |
| le poisson | fish |
| le poivre | pepper |
| le potage | soup |
| le poulet (rôti) | (roast) chicken |
| le repas | meal |
| le sel | salt |
| le sirop | syrup, concentrate |
| le souper | supper |
| le sucre | sugar |
| le thé | tea (*drink*) |
| le verre | glass |
| le vin | wine |

## * LA NOURRITURE ET LES REPAS

| | |
|---|---|
| une assiette | plate |
| la bière | beer |
| la boîte | tin, can; box |
| les bonbons | sweets |
| la bouteille | bottle |
| la crème* | cream |
| la cuiller, la cuillère | spoon |
| l'eau | water |
| les entrées* | entrées |
| la faim | hunger |
| la farine | flour |
| la fourchette | fork |
| les frites | chips, French fries |
| la glace* | ice cream |
| l'huile | oil |
| la limonade | lemonade |
| la nappe | table cloth |
| la nourriture | food |
| une omelette | omelette |
| les pommes frites | chips |
| la salade | salad |
| la sauce | sauce; gravy |
| la soif | thirst |
| la soucoupe | saucer |
| la soupe | soup |
| la tartine (de beurre) | piece of bread and butter |
| la tasse | cup |
| la vaisselle | dishes |
| la viande | meat |

manger to eat; boire to drink; avaler to swallow
déjeuner to have lunch; dîner to have dinner
souper to have supper; goûter to have tea; to taste
faire cuire/bouillir/frire to cook/boil/fry
la bière blonde lager
des tomates en boîte tinned tomatoes
une bouteille de vin a bottle of wine
des fraises à la crème strawberries and cream
eau gazeuse soda water; eau minérale mineral water

## ** LA NOURRITURE ET LES REPAS

| | |
|---|---|
| un appétit | appetite |
| le bouchon | cork |
| les chips | crisps |
| le 'coca' | 'Coke', coca cola |
| le cognac | brandy |
| les fruits de mer | seafood, shellfish |
| le goût | taste |
| le lard | bacon |
| le miel | honey |
| le pain au chocolat | *puff pastry bun filled with chocolate* |
| le pain grillé | toast |
| le petit pain | roll |
| le plateau* *(pl -x)* | tray |
| le porc* | pork |
| le pot à lait | milk jug |
| le riz | rice |
| le rosbif | roast beef |
| le sandwich | sandwich |
| le saucisson | (large) slicing sausage |
| le thermos | flask |
| un toast | slice *or* piece of toast |
| le veau* | veal |
| le vinaigre | vinegar |
| le whisky | whisky |
| le yaourt | yoghurt |

un café noir, un café nature black coffee
un café crème, un café au lait white coffee
un café express espresso coffee
le café filtre filter(ed) coffee
le café en poudre instant coffee
un chocolat chaud a hot chocolate (drink)
le chocolat au lait milk chocolate
le chocolat à croquer plain chocolate
mettre le couvert to set *or* lay the table
avant le déjeuner/le dîner before lunch/dinner
prendre son déjeuner to have lunch
j'ai eu du bœuf à déjeuner I had beef for lunch

## ** LA NOURRITURE ET LES REPAS

| | |
|---|---|
| la biscotte | toast (*in packets*) |
| la cafetière | coffee pot; coffee maker |
| la crème anglaise | custard |
| la crème Chantilly, la crème fouettée | whipped cream |
| la crêpe | pancake |
| la cuiller à thé *or* à café/à dessert/de service | teaspoon/dessert spoon/table spoon |
| les cuisses de grenouille | frogs' legs |
| la margarine | margarine |
| la paille | straw |
| les pâtes | pasta |
| la purée | mashed potatoes |
| les rillettes | potted meat (*made of pork or goose*) |
| la sauce vinaigrette | vinaigrette sauce |
| la saucisse | sausage |
| la théière | teapot |
| la volaille | poultry |

avoir (très) faim to be (very) hungry; j'ai une faim de loup! I'm ravenous!, I could eat a horse!

glace à la vanille/au café vanilla/coffee ice cream

une omelette aux champignons/au fromage a mushroom/cheese omelette

sauce à la menthe mint sauce

sauce tomate tomato sauce

avoir (très) soif to be (very) thirsty

une tartine au miel/à la confiture a slice *or* piece of bread and honey/bread and jam

une tasse à thé a teacup

une tasse à café a coffee cup

une tasse de thé/de café a cup of tea/coffee

faire la vaisselle to do the dishes *or* the washing-up

la viande hachée mince

une boisson alcoolisée/non alcoolisée an alcoholic drink/a soft drink

### *** LA NOURRITURE ET LES REPAS

| | |
|---|---|
| l'agneau | lamb (*meat*) |
| le bifteck | steak |
| le cacao | cocoa |
| le casse-croûte (*pl inv*) | snack |
| le champagne | champagne |
| le cidre | cider |
| le diplomate (à l'anglaise) | trifle |
| les escargots | snails |
| le foie | liver |
| le gibier | game |
| le glaçon* | ice cube |
| le 'haggis' | haggis |
| le :hamburger [ăbuʀgœʀ] | hamburger |
| le panaché | shandy |
| le ragoût | stew |
| les rognons | kidneys |
| le sucrier | sugar bowl |

des œufs au jambon ham and eggs, bacon and eggs
des œufs brouillés scrambled eggs
un œuf à la coque a (soft-)boiled egg
un œuf dur a hard-boiled egg
un œuf sur le plat a fried egg
un œuf poché a poached egg
un œuf de Pâques an Easter egg
le pain bis brown bread
le pain d'épice(s) gingerbread
'plat du jour' 'today's special'
du poisson frit avec des frites fish and chips
le thé au citron lemon tea
un verre d'eau/de vin a glass of water/of wine
bon appétit! have a nice meal!, enjoy your meal!
ça a bon goût it tastes good, it tastes nice
ça a mauvais goût it has a bad taste, it tastes
nasty
un sandwich au fromage/au jambon a cheese/ham
sandwich
le saucisson à l'ail garlic sausage

### *** LA NOURRITURE ET LES REPAS

| | |
|---|---|
| la **boisson** | drink |
| la **brioche** | bun |
| la **carafe d'eau** | jug of water |
| la **confiture** | jam |
| la **confiture d'orange** | |
| (*or* de citron *etc*) | marmalade |
| la **côtelette** | chop |
| la **cruche** | (milk) jug |
| la **gelée*** | jelly |
| une **infusion** | herb(al) tea |
| la **miette** | crumb |
| la **moule** | mussel |
| la **moutarde** | mustard |
| les **pommes allumette** | potato sticks |
| la **serviette*** | napkin, serviette |
| la **tisane** | herb(al) tea |
| la **tranche (de)** | slice (of) |
| les **tripes** | tripe |

### LE TABAC

LE TABAC (m)

| | | (f) LE TABAC | |
|---|---|---|---|
| le **briquet** | lighter | une **allumette** | match |
| le **cendrier** | ashtray | la **cigarette** | cigarette |
| le **cigare** | cigar | la **pipe** | pipe |
| le **tabac*** | tobacco | | |

une **boîte à allumettes** a matchbox
une **boîte d'allumettes** a box of matches
une **cigarette (à) bout filtre** a filter-tipped cigarette
**avez-vous du feu?** have you got a light?
**fumer la cigarette/le cigare/la pipe** to smoke
  cigarettes/cigars/a pipe
**'défense de fumer'** 'no smoking'
**allumer une cigarette/une pipe** *etc* to light a
  cigarette/a pipe *etc*
**éteindre une cigarette** to put out a cigarette
**arrêter de fumer** to give up smoking

## * LES OISEAUX

| | |
|---|---|
| le canard | duck |
| le coq | cock |
| le merle | blackbird |
| le moineau (*pl* -x) | sparrow |
| le nid | nest |
| un oiseau (*pl* -x) | bird |
| le pigeon | pigeon |
| le poulet | chicken |

## ** LES OISEAUX

| | |
|---|---|
| un aigle | eagle |
| le coucou | cuckoo |
| le hibou (*pl* -x) | owl |
| le perroquet | parrot |
| le rossignol | nightingale |
| le rouge-gorge | robin (red-breast) |
| le serin | canary |

## *** LES OISEAUX

| | |
|---|---|
| le bec | beak |
| le choucas | jackdaw |
| le coq de bruyère | grouse |
| le corbeau (*pl* -x) | raven |
| le cygne [sin] | swan |
| le dindon | turkey |
| un étourneau (*pl* -x) | starling |
| le faisan | pheasant |
| le faucon | falcon, hawk |
| le flamant (rose) | (pink) flamingo |
| le mainate | mynah bird |
| le martin-pêcheur | kingfisher |
| le paon [pã] | peacock |
| le pic* | woodpecker |
| le pingouin | penguin |
| le vautour | vulture |

**les oiseaux volent dans l'air** birds fly in the air
**ils battent des ailes** they flap their wings
**ils font des nids** they build nests

**\* LES OISEAUX**

| | |
|---|---|
| une alouette | lark |
| une oie | goose |
| la poule | hen |

**\*\* LES OISEAUX**

| | |
|---|---|
| une aile | wing |
| la corneille | crow, raven |
| la grive | thrush |
| l'hirondelle | swallow |
| la mouette | seagull |
| la perruche | budgie |
| la plume\* | feather |

**\*\*\* LES OISEAUX**

| | |
|---|---|
| une autruche | ostrich |
| la caille | quail |
| la cigogne | stork |
| la colombe | dove |
| la grouse | grouse |
| la mésange bleue | bluetit |
| la perdrix [pɛʀdʀi] | partridge |
| la pie | magpie |

**siffler** to whistle
**chanter** to sing
**la poule pond ses œufs dans la paille** the hen lays
  its eggs in the straw
**s'envoler** to fly away
**se poser** to come down, land
**à vol d'oiseau** as the crow flies

## * LES OUTILS

| | |
|---|---|
| les ciseaux | scissors |
| le clou | nail |
| le fil | thread |
| le fil de fer (barbelé) | (barbed) wire |
| le marteau *(pl -x)* | hammer |

## ** LES OUTILS

| | |
|---|---|
| un atelier | workshop |
| le bricolage | D.I.Y., do-it-yourself |
| le bricoleur | home handyman |
| le chantier | construction site |
| l'échafaudage | scaffolding |
| un élastique | rubber band, elastic band |
| un outil | tool |
| le pic* | pick, pickaxe |
| le pinceau *(pl -x)* | paintbrush |
| le râteau *(pl -x)* | rake |
| le ressort | spring |
| le scotch | sellotape, adhesive tape |

## *** LES OUTILS

| | |
|---|---|
| le cadenas | padlock |
| le ciseau *(pl -x)* | chisel |
| le décapsuleur | bottle-opener |
| le déplantoir | trowel *(for gardening)* |
| un escabeau *(pl -x)* | stepladder, pair of steps |
| un étau *(pl -x)* | vice |
| le foret | drill |
| le maillet | mallet |
| le marteau *(pl -x)* piqueur | pneumatic drill |
| le niveau *(pl -x)* à bulles | spirit level |
| un ouvre-boîte(s) *(pl ouvre-boîtes)* | tin opener |
| le rabot | plane |
| le tire-bouchon *(pl tire-bouchons)* | corkscrew |
| le tournevis | screwdriver |

**enfoncer un clou** to hammer in a nail
**'chantier interdit'** 'construction site: keep out'
**peindre** to paint; **tapisser** to paper

---

**\* LES OUTILS**

| | |
|---|---|
| la clef, la clé | key |
| une échelle | ladder |
| la machine | machine |

**\*\* LES OUTILS**

| | |
|---|---|
| une aiguille\* | needle |
| la bêche | spade |
| la corde\* | rope |
| la planche | plank |
| la punaise\* | drawing pin, thumbtack |
| la serrure | lock |
| la vis [vis] | screw |

**\*\*\* LES OUTILS**

| | |
|---|---|
| la binette | hoe |
| la boîte à outils | toolbox |
| la boîte à ouvrage | workbox |
| la clef anglaise | spanner |
| la colle\* | glue |
| la faux | scythe |
| la fourche | (garden) fork |
| la houe | hoe |
| la lime | file |
| la pelle\* | shovel |
| la perceuse | drill |
| les pinces | pliers |
| la pioche | pick, pickaxe |
| la scie | saw |
| la truelle | trowel (for building) |

**monter sur une échelle** to climb a ladder
**appuyer une échelle contre un mur** to lean a ladder against a wall
**accrocher des images avec du scotch/avec des punaises** to stick up pictures with sellotape/with drawing pins; **décrocher** to take down
**dévisser quelque chose** to unscrew something
**scier une planche en deux** to saw a plank in two

## * LES PARTIES DU CORPS

| | |
|---|---|
| le bras | arm |
| les cheveux | hair |
| le corps [kɔʀ] | body |
| le cou | neck |
| le doigt | finger |
| l'estomac [ɛstɔmɑ] | stomach |
| le genou (*pl* -x) | knee |
| le menton | chin |
| le nez | nose |
| un œil (*pl* yeux) | eye |
| un os [ɔs] (*pl* [o]) | bone |
| le pied | foot |
| le sang | blood |
| le visage | face |
| les yeux | eyes |

## ** LES PARTIES DU CORPS

| | |
|---|---|
| le cœur | heart |
| le côté | side |
| le dos | back |
| le front | forehead |
| le muscle | muscle |
| un ongle | nail |
| le talon | heel |

**se casser le bras/la jambe** to break one's arm/leg
**se faire couper les cheveux** to have one's hair cut
**montrer quelque chose du doigt** to point to something
**se moucher** to blow one's nose
**saigner du nez** to have a nose-bleed
**jeter un coup d'œil à quelqu'un** to glance at somebody
**en un clin d'œil** in the twinkling of an eye
**mouillé jusqu'aux os** soaked to the skin
**à pied** on foot
**un coup de pied** a kick
**marcher pieds nus** to walk barefoot
**marcher sur la pointe des pieds** to walk on tiptoe

## * LES PARTIES DU CORPS

| | |
|---|---|
| la bouche | mouth |
| la dent | tooth |
| la figure | face |
| la gorge | throat |
| la jambe | leg |
| la lèvre | lip |
| la main | hand |
| une oreille | ear |
| la peau | skin |
| la tête | head |
| la voix | voice |

## ** LES PARTIES DU CORPS

| | |
|---|---|
| la joue | cheek |
| la langue* | tongue |
| la paupière | eyelid |
| la poitrine | chest, bust |
| la taille* | figure; waist |
| la veine* | vein |

la peau douce/rêche soft/tough skin

parler à haute voix to speak loudly

parler à voix basse, parler à mi-voix to speak in a
low voice

de la tête aux pieds from head to foot

ils se sont serré la main they shook hands

être debout/assis(e)/couché(e)/à genoux to be stand-
ing/sitting/lying down/kneeling or on one's knees

s'agenouiller to kneel (down)

marcher dans l'eau jusqu'aux genoux to walk in
water up to one's knees

### *** LES PARTIES DU CORPS

| | |
|---|---|
| le cerveau | brain |
| le cil [sil] | eyelash |
| le coude | elbow |
| les doigts de pied | toes |
| le foie | liver |
| l'index | forefinger |
| le mollet | calf (of leg) |
| le gros orteil, l'orteil | the (big) toe |
| le poignet | wrist |
| le poing | fist |
| le pouce | thumb |
| le poumon | lung |
| le rein | kidney |
| le sein | breast |
| le sourcil [suRsi] | eyebrow |
| le squelette | skeleton |
| le teint | complexion |
| le trait | feature |
| le ventre | stomach |

son cœur battait his heart was beating
le côté gauche/le côté droit du corps the lefthand
 side/the righthand side of the body
à côté de moi, à mes côtés at my side
se couper les ongles to cut one's nails
un coup de poing a punch
à pleins poumons at the top of one's voice
froncer les sourcils to frown

**\*\*\* LES PARTIES DU CORPS**

| | |
|---|---|
| une artère | artery |
| la chair | flesh |
| la cheville | ankle |
| la colonne vertébrale | spine, backbone |
| la côte\* | rib |
| la cuisse | thigh |
| une épaule | shoulder |
| la hanche | hip |
| la mâchoire | jaw |
| la nuque | nape of the neck |
| la plante du pied | sole of the foot |
| la prunelle | pupil (of eye) |
| la tempe | temple |

**se fouler la cheville** to sprain one's ankle

**elle portait son sac à l'épaule** she was carrying her bag over her shoulder

**hausser les épaules** to shrug one's shoulders

**hocher la tête, faire un signe de tête affirmatif** to nod one's head

**hocher la tête, faire non de la tête** to shake one's head

**\* LES PAYS**

| | |
|---|---|
| les **États-Unis** | the United States |
| le **Marché commun** | the Common Market |
| le **pays\*** | country |

**\*\* LES PAYS**

| | |
|---|---|
| le **Canada** | Canada |
| le **pays de Galles** | Wales |
| le **Japon** | Japan |
| le **Luxembourg** | Luxemburg |
| le **Pakistan** | Pakistan |
| les **Pays-Bas** | the Netherlands |
| le **Portugal** | Portugal |

**\*\*\* LES PAYS**

| | |
|---|---|
| le **Brésil** | Brazil |
| le **Danemark** | Denmark |
| le **Maroc** | Morocco |
| le **Mexique** | Mexico |
| le **Viêt-nam** | Vietnam |

**mon pays natal** my native country
**la capitale de la France** the capital of France
**de quel pays venez-vous?** what country do you come from?
**je viens des États-Unis/du Canada/de la France** I come from the United States/from Canada/from France
**je suis aux Pays-Bas/au pays de Galles/en Italie** I am in the Netherlands/in Wales/in Italy
**je reviens des États-Unis/du Japon/de Belgique** I have just come back from the United States/from Japan/from Belgium
**envoyer une lettre aux Pays-Bas/au Portugal/en Angleterre** to send a letter to the Netherlands/to Portugal/to England
**les pays en voie de développement** the developing countries

**\* LES PAYS**

| | |
|---|---|
| l'Allemagne | Germany |
| l'Angleterre | England |
| la Belgique | Belgium |
| la Chine | China |
| l'Espagne | Spain |
| l'Europe | Europe |
| la France | France |
| la Grande-Bretagne | Great Britain |
| l'Italie | Italy |
| la Suisse | Switzerland |

**\*\* LES PAYS**

| | |
|---|---|
| l'Afrique | Africa |
| l'Afrique du Sud | South Africa |
| l'Amérique du Sud | South America |
| l'Asie | Asia |
| l'Australie | Australia |
| l'Écosse | Scotland |
| la Hollande | Holland |
| l'Inde | India |
| l'Irlande | Ireland |
| la Russie, l'U.R.S.S. | Union of Soviet Socialist Republics, Russia |

**\*\*\* LES PAYS**

| | |
|---|---|
| l'Algérie | Algeria |
| l'Autriche | Austria |
| la Corée | Korea |
| la Finlande | Finland |
| la Grèce | Greece |
| la Norvège | Norway |
| la Nouvelle Zélande | New Zealand |
| la Pologne | Poland |
| la Scandinavie | Scandinavia |
| la Suède | Sweden |
| la Tchécoslovaquie | Czechoslovakia |
| la Tunisie | Tunisia |
| la Turquie | Turkey |

## * LES POISSONS ET LES INSECTES

| | |
|---|---|
| l'air* | air |
| un insecte | insect |
| le papillon | butterfly |
| le poisson | fish |

## ** LES POISSONS ET LES INSECTES

| | |
|---|---|
| le cafard | beetle |
| les fruits de mer | shellfish, seafood |
| le grillon | cricket |
| le :haddock | haddock |
| le :hareng | herring |
| le merlan | whiting |
| le moustique | mosquito; midge |
| le papillon de nuit | moth |
| le poisson rouge | goldfish |
| le requin | shark |
| le saumon | salmon |
| le ver | worm |

## *** LES POISSONS ET LES INSECTES

| | |
|---|---|
| le brochet | pike |
| le criquet | cricket |
| le :homard | lobster |
| le poulpe | octopus |
| le thon | tuna fish, tunny fish |
| le ver à soie | silkworm |

aller à la pêche to go fishing
faire collection de papillons to collect butterflies

---

### * LES POISSONS ET LES INSECTES

| | |
|---|---|
| une abeille | bee |
| la guêpe | wasp |
| la mouche | fly |
| la queue* [kø] | tail |

### ** LES POISSONS ET LES INSECTES

| | |
|---|---|
| une aile | wing |
| la bête à bon dieu | ladybird |
| la fourmi | ant |
| la morue | cod |
| la moule | mussel |
| la puce | flea |
| la punaise* | bug |

### *** LES POISSONS ET LES INSECTES

| | |
|---|---|
| une anguille | eel |
| une araignée | spider |
| les branchies | gills |
| la chenille | caterpillar |
| la cigale | cicada |
| la coccinelle [kɔksinɛl] | ladybird |
| la crevette | shrimp |
| une écaille | scale |
| l'huître | oyster |
| la langouste | crawfish, crayfish |
| les langoustines | scampi |
| la libellule | dragonfly |
| la méduse | jellyfish |
| la mouche à vers | bluebottle |
| la nageoire | fin |
| la pieuvre | octopus |
| la sole | sole |
| la truite | trout |

---

une toile d'araignée a spider's web
l'abeille/la guêpe pique the bee/the wasp stings
nager to swim; voler to fly

\* LA POSTE

| | |
|---|---|
| le bureau (*pl* -x) de poste | post office |
| le cadran | dial |
| le courrier | mail, letters |
| un employé* | counter clerk |
| le facteur | postman |
| le formulaire | form |
| le guichet* | counter |
| le jeton | token (*for telephone*) |
| le mandat(-poste) | postal order |
| le nom | name |
| le numéro | number |
| le paquet | parcel |
| le récepteur | receiver (*part of telephone*) |
| les renseignements | information |
| le stylo | pen |
| le télégramme | telegram |
| le téléphone | telephone |
| le timbre*(-poste) | (postage) stamp |

**téléphoner à quelqu'un** to phone somebody
**donner un coup de fil à quelqu'un** to ring somebody
**un coup de téléphone** a (tele)phone call
**la tonalité** the dialling tone
**le signal d'appel** the ringing tone
**décrocher** to lift the receiver
**composer le numéro** to dial
**raccrocher** to hang up
**on m'a coupé** I've been cut off
**distribuer le courrier** to deliver the mail

\* LA POSTE

| | |
|---|---|
| une adresse | address |
| la boîte aux lettres\* | letterbox; postbox, pillar box |
| la cabine téléphonique | callbox |
| la carte postale | postcard |
| la distribution\* | delivery (of mail) |
| une enveloppe | envelope |
| la fiche | form |
| l'horloge parlante | the speaking clock, TIM |
| la lettre | letter |
| la levée | collection (of mail) |
| la majuscule | block or capital letter |
| la poste\* | post office; post |
| la poste aérienne | airmail |
| la réponse | reply |
| la sacoche\* | mailbag, postbag |

à l'heure de pointe at the peak period
envoyer quelque chose par la poste to send something by post or through the post
mettre une lettre à la poste to post a letter
recevoir to receive
renvoyer to send back
faire suivre to forward
par avion by airmail
remplir une fiche or une formule to fill in a form
en majuscules in block or capital letters

**\*\* LA POSTE**

| | |
|---|---|
| un **aérogramme** | airmail letter |
| un **annuaire du téléphone**, | |
| le **Bottin** | telephone directory |
| le **colis** | parcel, packet |
| les **fils** [fil] | wires |
| le **papier à lettres** | writing paper |

**\*\*\* LA POSTE**

| | |
|---|---|
| un **abonné** | subscriber |
| l'**annuaire des** | |
| **professions** | the Yellow Pages |
| le **code postal** | postal code |
| le **destinataire** | addressee |
| l'**expéditeur** | sender |
| les **imprimés** | printed matter |
| le **papier gris**, le **papier d'emballage** | |
| brown paper, wrapping paper | |
| le **port**\* | postage |
| le **poteau** (pl -x) | |
| **télégraphique** | telegraph pole |
| le **standardiste** | (telephone) operator, telephonist |

**sous ce pli** enclosed, herewith
**allô** hello (on phone)
**qui est à l'appareil?** who's speaking?
**c'est de la part de qui?** who's speaking?
**ici Charles** this is Charles
**'lui-même', 'c'est moi'** 'speaking'
**la ligne est occupée** the line is engaged
**ne quittez pas** hold the line please

## ** LA POSTE

| | |
|---|---|
| la bande* | wrapper |
| la carte-lettre | |
| (*pl* cartes-lettres) | letter-card |
| la lettre | |
| recommandée | registered letter |

## *** LA POSTE

| | |
|---|---|
| la communication | |
| interurbaine | trunk call |
| la communication | |
| locale | local call |
| la dépêche | wire, telegram |
| la standardiste | (telephone) operator, telephonist |

amitiés *very best wishes or* regards
bien affectueusement (à vous) *yours affectionately*
bien amicalement *or* cordialement (à vous) *yours ever*
bons baisers *love and kisses*
veuillez agréer mes (*or* nos) salutations distinguées *yours faithfully*
je vous prie d'agréer, Monsieur (*or* Madame *etc*)
l'expression de mes sentiments les meilleurs *yours sincerely*

\* LES PROFESSIONS ET LES MÉTIERS

| | |
|---|---|
| un **agent** (de police) | policeman |
| un **architecte** [aʀʃitɛktə] | architect |
| un **artiste** | artist |
| le **camionneur** | lorry driver |
| le **collègue** | colleague |
| le **concierge** | caretaker; janitor |
| le **constructeur** (de maisons) | builder |
| le **curé** | parish priest |
| le **douanier** | customs officer |
| un **écrivain** | writer |
| un **électricien** | electrician |
| un **emploi** | job |
| un **employé**\* | employee; clerk |
| un **employeur** | employer |
| un **ingénieur** | engineer |
| le **journaliste** | journalist |
| le **juge** | judge |
| le **marin** | sailor; seaman |
| le **métier** | trade |
| le **mineur** | miner |
| un **ouvrier** | worker |
| le **patron**\* | boss |
| le **photographe** | photographer |
| le **pilote**\* | pilot; racing driver |
| le **pompier** | fireman |
| le **président** | president; chairman |
| le **prince** | prince |
| le **professeur** | teacher |
| le **reporter** [ʀəpɔʀtɛʀ] | reporter |
| le **roi** | king |
| le **sapeur-pompier** | fireman |
| le **secrétaire**\* | secretary |
| le **soldat** | soldier |
| le **travail** | work |

**faire une demande d'emploi** to apply for a job
**un homme de métier** a specialist, an expert
**il est plombier de son métier** he is a plumber by trade or to trade

## \* LES PROFESSIONS ET LES MÉTIERS

| | |
|---|---|
| une **artiste** | artist |
| la **coiffeuse\*** | hairdresser |
| la **concierge** | caretaker |
| la **cuisinière\*** | cook |
| une **employée** | employee |
| la **femme de ménage** | cleaning woman |
| la **grève** | strike |
| une **infirmière** | nurse |
| la **journaliste** | journalist |
| une **ouvrière** | worker |
| la **patronne\*** | boss |
| la **présidente** | president; chairwoman |
| la **princesse** | princess |
| la **profession** | profession |
| la **reine** | queen |
| la **secrétaire\*** | secretary |
| la **vedette\*** | star |
| la **vendeuse** | salesgirl, shop assistant |

**que faites-vous dans la vie?** what work do you do?,
   what is your job?
**être engagé** to be taken on
**être renvoyé** to be dismissed
**gagner 100 livres par semaine** to earn £100 per
   week
**se mettre en grève** to go on strike

## ** LES PROFESSIONS ET LES MÉTIERS

| | |
|---|---|
| un auteur | author |
| le balayeur | street sweeper |
| le charpentier | joiner |
| le chauffeur de taxi | taxi driver |
| le commerçant | tradesman |
| le comptable | accountant |
| le couturier | fashion designer |
| le député | M.P., member of parliament |
| le dessinateur | designer |
| le fonctionnaire | civil servant |
| le gréviste | striker |
| l'homme d'affaires | businessman |
| l'homme de la loi | lawyer |
| l'homme politique | politician |
| un interprète | interpreter |
| le mannequin* | model (*person*) |
| le manœuvre | (industrial) labourer |
| le menuisier | joiner |
| le ministère | ministry (in politics) |
| le ministre | (government) minister |
| le pasteur | minister |
| le peintre | painter |
| le personnel | staff |
| le poète | poet |
| le premier ministre | Prime Minister |
| le prêtre | priest |
| le psychologue [psikɔlɔg] | psychologist |
| le représentant (de commerce) | representative |
| le salaire | salary, pay, wages |
| le spécialiste | specialist |
| le traitement | salary |

**se mettre au travail** to start work, get down to work

**travailler pour gagner sa vie** to work to earn one's living

## ** LES PROFESSIONS ET LES MÉTIERS

| | |
|---|---|
| l'administration | administration |
| les affaires* | business |
| la carrière* | career |
| la compagnie | company |
| la couturière | dressmaker |
| la dispute | argument, dispute |
| une entreprise | business |
| la femme-agent | policewoman |
| la firme | firm |
| la formation | training |
| une interprète | interpreter |
| la maison de commerce | firm |
| une ouvreuse | usherette |
| la réceptionniste | receptionist |

## *** LES PROFESSIONS ET LES MÉTIERS

| | |
|---|---|
| un **apprenti** | apprentice |
| un **apprentissage** | apprenticeship |
| un **avocat*** | barrister |
| un **avoué** | solicitor |
| le **cadre*** | executive |
| le **chirurgien** | surgeon |
| le **chômeur** | unemployed person |
| le **clochard** | tramp |
| le **cosmonaute** | cosmonaut, astronaut |
| un **éditeur** | publisher |
| le **gérant** | manager |
| le **laveur de vitres** | window cleaner |
| le **maçon** | mason |
| le **médecin vétérinaire** | vet(erinary surgeon) |
| le **moine** | monk |
| le **nettoyeur de vitres** | window cleaner |
| un **opérateur** | cameraman |
| le **président-directeur général, le P.D.G.** | managing director |
| le **ramoneur** | chimney sweep |
| le **savant** | scientist |
| le **speaker** [spikœr] | announcer |
| le **stage** | (training) course |
| le **stagiaire** | trainee |
| le **syndicat** | trade union |
| les **syndiqués** | union members |
| le **vétérinaire** | vet |
| le **vigneron** | wine grower |

une **augmentation de salaire** a wage rise
être en **chômage** to be out of work, to be unemployed
être au **chômage** to be on the dole
mettre quelqu'un au **chômage** to make somebody redundant
faire un **stage** to go on a (training) course

### *** LES PROFESSIONS ET LES MÉTIERS

| | |
|---|---|
| la **dactylo(graphe)** | typist |
| la **gérante** | manageress |
| la **grève perlée** | go-slow |
| la **grève du zèle** | work-to-rule |
| la **religieuse** | nun |
| la **speakerine** | |
| [spikin] | announcer |
| la **sténo-dactylo(graphe)** | shorthand typist |

## LES SALUTATIONS                    GREETINGS
**bonjour** hello; good morning; good afternoon
**salut** hello, hi; goodbye
**ça va?** how are you?, how's things?
**ça va!** (*in reply*) fine!
**enchanté(e)** (very) pleased to meet you
**allô** hello (*on telephone*)
**bonsoir** good evening, hello; good night
**bonne nuit** good night (*when going to bed*)
**au revoir** goodbye
**à demain** see you tomorrow
**à bientôt, à tout à l'heure** see you later
**adieu** goodbye, farewell

## MEILLEURS VŒUX                    BEST WISHES
**bon anniversaire** happy birthday
**bonne fête** happy 'saint's day'
**joyeux Noël** merry Christmas
**bonne année** happy New Year
**joyeuses Pâques** happy Easter
**meilleurs vœux** best wishes
**félicitations** congratulations
**bon appétit** have a nice meal, enjoy your meal
**bon courage** all the best, chin up
**bonne chance** good luck
**à tes** (*or* **vos**) **souhaits** bless you (*after a sneeze*)
**à la tienne** (*or* **la vôtre**) cheers
**à ta** (*or* **votre**) **santé** good health

| ÉTONNEMENT | SURPRISE |
|---|---|

**mon Dieu** my goodness
**eh bien, eh ben** well
**comment?, hein?, eh?, quoi?** what (was that)?
**ah bon** oh, I see
**ça, par exemple** well, well; my word; really
**que de . . .** what a lot of . . .
**sans blague(?)** really(?)
**ah oui?, c'est vrai?, vraiment?** really?
**tu rigoles, tu plaisantes** you're kidding *or* joking
**quelle chance!** what a stroke of luck!
**tiens!** well, well!

| POLITESSE | POLITENESS |
|---|---|

**s'il vous (*or* te) plaît** please; excuse me (*when approaching stranger*)
**merci** thank you; no, thank you
**non merci** no thank you; **oui merci** yes please
**de rien, je vous en prie, il n'y a pas do quoi** not at all, it's quite all right, don't mention it
**volontiers** willingly, with pleasure

| ACCORD | AGREEMENT |
|---|---|

**oui** yes
**mais oui, bien sûr** of course
**d'accord** O.K., all right
**bon, bien** fine, O.K.
**c'est entendu(?)** agreed(?)
**soit!** [swat] so be it, agreed
**justement** exactly, that's just it
**tant mieux** so much the better
**ça m'est égal** I don't mind, it's all the same to me

## DÉSACCORD DISAGREEMENT

**non** no; **ah non alors**! oh no!, no no!
**mais non** no (*contradicting a positive statement*)
**si, mais si** yes (*contradicting a negative statement*)
**bien sûr que non** of course not
**jamais de la vie** never, not on your life
**pas du tout** not at all, far from it
**au contraire** on the contrary
**tant pis** too bad
**oh mais non, vraiment** really (*exasperated*)
**ça, par exemple** well I never, well really
**quel culot, quel toupet** what a cheek, what a nerve
**mêlez-vous de vos affaires** mind your own
  business
**cela dépend** that depends, it all depends
**quand même** even so; really (*exasperated*), that's
  a bit much
**à bas . . .** down with . . .

## DÉTRESSE DISTRESS

**au secours** help; **aïe** ouch, ow
**hélas** alas, oh dear
**pardon** (I'm) sorry, excuse me, I beg your pardon
**je m'excuse** I'm sorry (*for having done*)
**je regrette** I'm sorry
**désolé(e)** I'm (really) sorry
**c'est dommage, quel dommage** what a pity
**zut, flûte** drat, dash, bother; **mince alors** dash it
**j'en ai marre** I'm fed up with it
**c'en est trop** it's (just) too much
**je n'en peux plus** I can't stand it any more
**oh là là** oh dear
**quelle horreur** what a thought; how awful
**que faire?** what shall I (*or* we) do?
**à quoi bon . . .** (+ *infinitive*) what's the use of . . .?
**quelle barbe** what a nuisance
**que je suis (fatigué** *etc*) how (tired *etc*) I am
**c'est embêtant (de . . .)** it's embarrassing (to . . .)
**ça m'embête** it bothers me
**ça m'agace** it annoys me, it gets on my nerves

## LES ORDRES                                    ORDERS
**attention** watch, be careful
**halte-là** stop
**hep** or **eh, vous là-bas** hey, you there
**fiche-moi le camp** clear off, clear out
**chut** shhhh
**ça suffit** that's enough
**défense de (fumer** *etc*) no (smoking *etc*)
**doucement** gently, go easy, easy does it
**allons** go on, come on
**allons-y** let's go
**allez-y, vas-y** on you go, go on, go ahead

## AUTRES                                        OTHERS
**ah bon** oh well, O.K.
**et alors** well (*threatening*); so what?, so?
**eh bien . . .** well . . .
**aucune idée** no idea
**peut-être** perhaps, maybe
**je ne sais pas** I don't know
**vous désirez?** can I help you?
**voici, tiens** (or **tenez**) here, here you are ·
**voilà** there, there you are
**j'arrive** just coming
**ne t'en fais pas** don't worry
**ce n'est pas la peine** it's not worth it
**à propos** by the way
**dis donc** (or **dites donc**) listen, I say
**chéri(e)** darling
**le** (or **la**) **pauvre** poor thing

* LA SANTÉ

| | |
|---|---|
| le cachet | tablet |
| le cachet d'aspirine | aspirin |
| le choc | shock |
| le comprimé | tablet |
| le dentiste | dentist |
| le docteur | doctor |
| l'hôpital (*pl* hôpitaux) | hospital |
| un infirmier | (male) nurse |
| le mal | ache |
| le malade | patient |
| le médecin | doctor |
| le médicament | medicine, drug |
| le pharmacien | chemist |
| le rhume (de cerveau) | cold (in the head) |
| le sang | blood |
| le sommeil | sleep |
| le sparadrap | sticking plaster |

se sentir bien/malade to feel well/ill
être bien portant *or* en bonne santé to be in good
  health
à l'hôpital in hospital; to hospital
le médecin de service the doctor on duty
se faire du mal to hurt oneself
se casser le bras/la jambe to break one's arm/leg
le médecin soigne ses malades, le médecin s'occupe
  de ses malades the doctor looks after his patients
avoir mal aux dents/mal à la tête/mal au ventre
  to have toothache/a headache/a stomach ache
avoir mal à la gorge to have a sore throat
ça me fait mal au cœur it makes me feel sick
il va mieux maintenant he is getting better now
maigrir to lose weight
grossir to put on weight
j'ai sommeil I feel sleepy, I'm tired
je suis enrhumé I've got a cold

**\* LA SANTÉ**

| | |
|---|---|
| une **ambulance** | ambulance |
| une **angine** | tonsillitis |
| une **appendicite** | appendicitis |
| la **bande**\* | bandage |
| la **blessure** | injury, wound |
| la **crème**\* | cream, ointment |
| la **douleur** | pain |
| la **fièvre** | fever, (high) temperature |
| la **force** | strength, force |
| la **grippe** | flu, influenza |
| une **infirmière** | nurse |
| les **lunettes** | glasses |
| la **maladie** | illness |
| la **médecine** | (science of) medicine |
| une **ordonnance**\* | prescription |
| la **pilule** | pill |
| la **santé** | health |
| la **température** | temperature |
| la **toux** | cough |

**avoir chaud/froid** to be hot/cold
**tousser** to cough; **éternuer** to sneeze
**avoir** or **faire de la température** to have a temperature
**être crispé de douleur** to be twisted or contorted with pain
**vomir** to vomit, be sick
**de toutes ses forces** with all one's strength
**hors d'haleine** out of breath, breathless
**guérir** to cure; **être guéri** to be cured
**se rétablir** to recover
**faible** weak; **faibli** weakened
**garder le lit** to stay in bed
**gémir** to moan, groan
**s'évanouir** to faint
**évanoui** unconscious
**perdre/reprendre connaissance** to lose/regain consciousness
**enflé** swollen; **pénible** painful

## ** LA SANTÉ

| | |
|---|---|
| le bandage | bandage |
| le bleu* | bruise |
| le brancard | stretcher |
| un coup de soleil | sunstroke |
| le fauteuil roulant | wheelchair |
| le nerf | nerve |
| un œil (*pl* yeux) poché | black eye |
| le plâtre* | plaster, plaster cast |
| le poison | poison |
| les premiers soins | first aid |
| le régime | diet |
| le repos | rest |
| le rhume des foins | hayfever |

## *** LA SANTÉ

| | |
|---|---|
| un abcès | abscess |
| un accès | fit |
| le cabinet de consultation | surgery |
| le cancer | cancer |
| le coton hydrophile | cotton wool |
| le dentier | (set of) false teeth |
| le fortifiant | tonic |
| le microbe | germ |
| les oreillons | mumps |
| le pansement | dressing, bandage |
| le pouls [pu] | pulse |
| le refroidissement | chill |
| le remède | remedy, cure |
| le stéthoscope | stethoscope |
| le vertige | giddiness |

**se reposer** to rest, have a rest
**souffrir de** to suffer from
**il a attrapé un microbe pendant ses vacances** he picked up a bug on holiday
**ça me tape sur les nerfs** it gets on my nerves
**prendre le pouls à quelqu'un** to feel somebody's pulse
**je te souhaite un prompt rétablissement** get well soon

## ** LA SANTÉ

| | |
|---|---|
| une ampoule | blister |
| la cicatrice | scar |
| la clinique | clinic, hospital |
| une écharpe* | sling |
| une épidémie | epidemic |
| la langue* | tongue |
| la nausée | sickness, vomiting |
| la radio(graphie) | X-ray |
| la respiration | breathing |
| la salle d'hôpital | ward |
| la salle d'opération | operating theatre |

## *** LA SANTÉ

| | |
|---|---|
| la béquille | crutch |
| la contusion | bruise |
| la coqueluche | whooping cough |
| la crise cardiaque | heart attack |
| une écharde | splinter |
| une égratignure | scratch |
| la guérison | recovery |
| une intervention | operation |
| la maison de retraite | old folks' home |
| la meurtrissure | bruise |
| la migraine | migraine |
| l'ouate (hydrophile) | cotton wool |
| la piqûre* | injection; sting |
| la plaie | wound |
| la pommade | ointment |
| la rechute | relapse |
| la rougeole | measles |
| la rubéole | German measles |
| la sueur | sweat |
| la transfusion sanguine | blood transfusion |
| la typhoïde | typhoid |
| la varicelle | chickenpox |
| la variole | smallpox |

se faire opérer (de l'appendicite) to have an
operation (for appendicitis)

\* LES SPORTS

| | |
|---|---|
| un adversaire | opponent |
| un arbitre\* | (*football*, *rugby*) referee; (*tennis*) umpire |
| le badminton | badminton |
| le ballon\* | (foot)ball |
| le basket(ball) | basketball |
| le billard | billiards |
| le but\* [byt] | goal |
| le camping\* | camping; camp-site |
| le champion | champion |
| le cricket | cricket |
| le cyclisme | cycling |
| le débutant | beginner |
| l'entraînement | training |
| un entraîneur | trainer, coach |
| le football | football |
| le gardien (de but) | (goal)keeper |
| le golf | golf |
| le jeu\* (*pl* -x) | game; play |
| le joueur | player |
| le maillot\* | (football) jersey |
| le match | game, match |
| le netball | netball |
| le patin (à roulettes) | (roller) skate |
| le résultat | result |
| le rugby | rugby |
| le score | score |
| le service | service |
| le ski\* | skiing; ski |
| le spectateur | spectator |
| le sport | sport |
| le stade | stadium |
| le tennis\* | tennis; tennis court |
| le terrain\* (de sports) | ground; pitch; course |
| le volley-ball | volleyball |

jouer au football/au tennis to play football/tennis
marquer un but to score a goal
faire du ski to ski, go skiing

**\* LES SPORTS**

| | |
|---|---|
| l'attaque | attack |
| une auberge de jeunesse | youth hostel |
| une avance (de) | lead (of) (*distance, time*) |
| la balle | ball (*for tennis etc*); bullet |
| la boule | bowl (*used in game of bowls*); billiards ball |
| la championne | champion |
| la compétition | competition |
| la coupe | cup |
| la course\* | running; racing; race |
| une équipe | team |
| la finale | final |
| la mi-temps | half-time |
| la natation | swimming |
| une ouverture | opening |
| la pêche\* | fishing |
| la pétanque | (type of) bowls |
| la piscine | swimming pool |
| la piste\* | track; run |
| la première mi-temps | the first half |
| la promenade\* | walk |
| la raquette | racket |
| la réunion | meeting |

**prendre part à** *or* **assister à une compétition** to take part in a competition
**sportif** fond of sports; athletic
**mener** to be leading (*in match*)
**être en tête** to be in the lead
**prendre la tête** to take the lead
**aller passer ses vacances en auberges de jeunesse** to go youth-hostelling
**aller à la pêche** to go fishing
**la canne à pêche** the fishing rod

## ** LES SPORTS

| | |
|---|---|
| l'alpinisme | climbing, mountaineering |
| un alpiniste | climber, mountaineer |
| le concours* | competition |
| le concurrent | competitor |
| le coup de pied | kick |
| le court (de tennis) | (tennis) court |
| le filet* | net |
| le gagnant | winner |
| le:hockey | hockey |
| le patinage | skating |
| le perdant | loser |
| le ping-pong | table tennis |
| le poteau (pl -x) | goal post |
| le poteau d'arrivée | winning post |
| le record mondial | world record |
| le sac de couchage | sleeping bag |
| le set | set (tennis) |
| le ski nautique | water skiing |
| les sports athlétiques | athletics |
| les sports d'hiver | winter sports |
| le supporter | |
| [sypɔrtɛr] | supporter |
| le tennis de table | table tennis |
| le tournoi | tournament |

faire de l'alpinisme to go climbing or mountaineering
gagner/perdre un match to win/lose a game
un match nul a draw
ils ont fait match nul they drew
marquer des points to score (points)
marquer les points to keep the score

## ** LES SPORTS

| | |
|---|---|
| la chasse | hunting |
| la chasse au renard | fox-hunting |
| une course contre la montre | time trial |
| les courses de chevaux | horse-racing |
| la défense* | defence |
| une éliminatoire | heat |
| une étape | lap |
| la gagnante | winner |
| la mêlée | scrum |
| une paire de tennis | pair of tennis shoes or gym shoes |
| la partie* | game |
| la perdante | loser |
| la rencontre* | match |
| la reprise | round |
| la réunion hippique | race meeting |
| la station de sports d'hiver | winter sports resort |
| la touche* | touch |
| la tribune | stand |

s'échauffer to warm up
s'entraîner to train
professionnel professional
amateur amateur
battre, vaincre to beat, defeat
battre quelqu'un (par) 6 à 3 to beat somebody 6-3
battre quelqu'un à plate(s) couture(s) to beat somebody hollow
franchir la ligne d'arrivée to cross the finishing line

*** LES SPORTS

| | |
|---|---|
| l'athlétisme | athletics |
| le canotage | rowing |
| le catch | wrestling |
| le champ de course | race course |
| le championnat | championship |
| le chronomètre | stopwatch |
| le chronométreur | timekeeper |
| le détenteur (du titre) | (title-)holder |
| le double mixte | mixed doubles |
| le footing | jogging |
| le gymnase | gymnasium, gym |
| l'hippisme | horse-racing |
| le javelot | javelin |
| les Jeux olympiques | the Olympic Games |
| le plongeon | dive |
| le rallye (automobile) | (car) rally |
| le saut en hauteur | high jump |
| le saut en longueur | long jump |
| le simple-messieurs | men's singles |
| le tir | shooting |
| le tir à l'arc | archery |
| le vol libre | hang-gliding |

**lancer** to throw; **courir** to run; **sauter** to jump
**donner un coup de pied à** to kick
**faire du footing** to go jogging

### *** LES SPORTS

| | |
|---|---|
| la barre transversale | cross-bar |
| la boxe | boxing |
| la canne* | golf club |
| la course à l'aviron | boat race |
| une échappée | sudden spurt |
| égalité | deuce |
| l'équitation | horse-riding |
| l'escrime | fencing |
| la luge | sledge, toboggan |
| la lutte | wrestling |
| la lutte à la corde | tug-of-war |
| la passe (en avant) | (forward) pass |
| la patinoire | ice rink |
| la pelouse* | pitch, field, ground |
| la prolongation | extra time |

jouer les prolongations to play extra time

**\* LE TEMPS QU'IL FAIT**

| | |
|---|---|
| l'air\* | air |
| un arc-en-ciel | |
| (*pl* arcs-en-ciel) | rainbow |
| le bonhomme de niege | snowman |
| le brouillard | fog |
| le ciel | sky |
| le coup de tonnerre | thunderclap |
| le coup de vent | gust of wind |
| le courant d'air | draught |
| un éclair | flash of lightning |
| le froid | cold |
| le monde | world |
| un orage | thunderstorm |
| le parapluie | umbrella |
| le soleil\* | sun |
| le temps\* | weather |
| le tonnerre | thunder |
| le vent | wind |

**quel temps fait-il?** what's the weather like?
**il fait chaud/froid** it's hot/cold
**il fait beau** it's a lovely day
**il fait mauvais (temps)** it's a horrible day
**il fait frais** it is cool
**il fait du soleil/du vent** it's sunny/windy
**en plein air** in the open air
**il fait jour/nuit** it's daytime/night-time
**il fait du brouillard** it's foggy
**il y avait des éclairs** there were flashes of lightning, lightning flashed
**comme un éclair** like a flash, like greased lightning
**en un éclair** in a flash
**le temps est à l'orage** there is thunder in the air
**le tonnerre gronde** the thunder roars

**\* LE TEMPS QU'IL FAIT**

| | |
|---|---|
| la **boule de neige** | snowball |
| la **chaleur** | heat |
| une **étoile** | star |
| la **foudre** | lightning |
| la **fumée** | smoke |
| la **glace**\* | ice |
| une **inondation** | flood |
| la **lumière** | light |
| la **lune** | moon |
| la **neige** | snow |
| une **ombre** | shadow |
| la **pluie** | rain |
| la **saison** | season |
| la **température** | temperature |

le **coup de foudre** flash of lightning; love at first sight

la **fumée monte en l'air** the smoke rises up into the air

**Paris sous la neige** Paris in the snow

il **neige** it's snowing

à **l'ombre** in the shadow, in the shade

**pleuvoir (fort)** to rain (hard)

il **pleut** it's raining

il **pleut à verse** it's pouring (with rain)

le **soleil brille** the sun is shining

au **soleil** in the sunshine

le **vent souffle** the wind is blowing

**mourir de froid** to freeze to death

il **gèle** it's freezing

il **dégèle** it's thawing

**fondre** to melt

**frappé par la foudre, foudroyé** struck by lightning

**orageux** thundery

**humide** humid; damp

**mouillé** wet

se **mouiller** to get wet

se **mouiller les pieds** to get one's feet wet

## ** LE TEMPS QU'IL FAIT

| | |
|---|---|
| le bulletin de la météo | weather report |
| le climat | climate |
| le crépuscule | twilight |
| le gel, le givre | frost |
| le nuage | cloud |
| le parasol | parasol |
| le paratonnerre | lightning conductor |
| le smog | smog |

## *** LE TEMPS QU'IL FAIT

| | |
|---|---|
| un amoncellement de neige | snowdrift |
| le baromètre | barometer |
| le chasse-neige (pl inv) | snowplough |
| le clair de lune | moonlight |
| le coucher du soleil | sunset |
| les dégâts | damage, destruction |
| le dégel | thaw |
| le déluge | deluge, flood |
| le flocon de neige | snowflake |
| les frimas | wintry weather |
| le glaçon* | icicle |
| le lever du soleil | sunrise |
| un ouragan | hurricane |
| le point de congélation | freezing point |
| le rayon* de soleil | ray of sunshine |
| le tremblement de terre | earthquake |
| le verglas | black ice |

le ciel est nuageux/couvert the sky is cloudy/ overcast
au coucher/au lever du soleil at sunset/sunrise
le soleil se lève/se couche the sun rises/sets

## ** LE TEMPS QU'IL FAIT

| | |
|---|---|
| l'atmosphère | atmosphere |
| la chute de neige | snowfall |
| l'espace | space |
| la flaque d'eau | puddle |
| la gelée* | frost |
| la neige fondue | sleet; slush |
| l'obscurité | darkness |
| la poussière | dust |
| les prévisions météorologiques | weather forecast |
| la tempête | tempest, gale, storm |
| les ténèbres | darkness |

## *** LE TEMPS QU'IL FAIT

| | |
|---|---|
| l'aube | dawn |
| une averse | shower, downpour |
| la bise | cold north wind |
| la brise | breeze |
| la brume | mist |
| la canicule | heatwave |
| la congère | snowdrift |
| la coulée (de neige) | flurry (of snow) |
| une éclaircie | bright period |
| les fleurs de givre | frost patterns (on window) |
| la goutte de pluie | raindrop |
| la grêle | hail |
| la lueur | light |
| la rafale | squall |
| la rosée | dew |
| la sécheresse | drought |
| la vague de chaleur | heatwave |

une plaque de verglas a patch of black ice
rude harsh; doux (f douce) mild
je suis gelé or glacé I'm freezing or frozen
j'ai les mains gelées or glacées my hands are freezing or frozen
être gelé jusqu'aux os to be frozen stiff

## * LE THÉÂTRE

| | |
|---|---|
| un **acteur** | actor |
| le **billet** | ticket |
| le **costume**\* | costume |
| le **décor**\* | scenery |
| le **foyer** | foyer |
| le **guichet**\* | box office |
| le **maquillage** | make-up |
| un **orchestre**\* | orchestra; (seat in the) stalls |
| le **personnage** | character, person (*in play*) |
| le **programme** | programme (*leaflet*) |
| le **rideau** (*pl* -x) | curtain |
| le **rôle** | role, part |
| le **spectacle** | show |
| le **spectateur** | member of the audience |
| le **texte** | text; lines |
| le **théâtre** | theatre |

les **trois coups** the three knocks (*announcing beginning of play*)

le **rideau se lève et retombe** the curtain rises and falls again

**jouer le rôle de** to play the part of

un **fauteuil d'orchestre** a seat in the stalls

**apprendre son texte par cœur** to learn one's lines by heart

**j'ai eu un trou (de mémoire)** my mind went blank

**avoir le trac** to get stage fright

## * LE THÉÂTRE

| | |
|---|---|
| une actrice | actress |
| une affiche | notice; poster |
| la comédie | comedy |
| une entrée* | entrance |
| la musique | music |
| la pièce* (de théâtre) | play |
| la place* | seat |
| la représentation | performance |
| la salle* | house; audience |
| la scène* | stage; scene |
| la séance | performance; showing |
| la sortie | exit, way out |
| la tragédie | tragedy |
| la vedette* | star |

bis! encore!
remboursé! give us our money back!
réserver des places to book seats
entrer sur (la) scène to go or come onstage
sortir de scène to leave the stage, go or come
offstage

## ** LE THÉÂTRE

| | |
|---|---|
| les applaudissements | applause |
| un auditoire | audience |
| le balcon* | dress circle |
| le cercle dramatique | dramatic society |
| le jeu* | acting |
| le metteur en scène | producer |
| un opéra | opera |
| le projecteur | spotlight |
| le public | audience |
| le scénario | script |
| le souffleur | prompter |

## *** LE THÉÂTRE

| | |
|---|---|
| le dramaturge | playwright, dramatist |
| un entr'acte | interval |
| le parterre* | stalls |
| le poulailler* | 'the gods' |
| le producteur | (film) producer |
| le régisseur | stage manager |
| le vestiaire | cloakroom |

**les acteurs s'inclinent** the actors bow
**l'auditoire applaudit** the audience applaud
**pendant l'entr'acte** during the interval
**au vestiaire** to the cloakroom; in the cloakroom

## ** LE THÉÂTRE

| | |
|---|---|
| la distribution* | cast (*on programme*) |
| une estrade | platform |
| la farce | farce |
| la location* | booking |
| la loge* | box |
| la mise en scène | production |
| une ouvreuse | usherette, attendant |

## *** LE THÉÂTRE

| | |
|---|---|
| la corbeille* | circle |
| les coulisses | wings |
| la critique | review; the critics |
| la fosse (d'orchestre) | (orchestra) pit |
| une intrigue | plot |
| les jumelles* de théâtre | opera glasses |
| la pièce à sensation | thriller |
| la rampe | footlights |
| la répétition | rehearsal |
| la répétition générale | dress rehearsal |

**\* LES VÉHICULES**

| | |
|---|---|
| un autobus | bus |
| un autocar | coach |
| un avion (à réaction) | (jet) plane |
| le ballon* | balloon |
| le bateau (*pl* -x) | boat |
| le bus | bus |
| le camion | lorry, truck |
| le canot | rowing boat |
| le car | coach |
| le cyclomoteur | moped |
| l'hélicoptère | helicopter |
| l'hovercraft | hovercraft |
| le navire | ship |
| le prix du billet | fare (*any mode of transport*) |
| le prix du ticket | fare (*boat, plane*) |
| le scooter | scooter |
| le train | train |
| le vélo | bike |
| le vélomoteur | moped |

voyager to travel
faire un voyage à to go on a journey to
il est allé à Paris en avion he went to Paris by air *or* by plane, he flew to Paris
par avion by airmail
monter en ballon to go up in a balloon
aller en bateau to go by boat, sail
le canot pneumatique inflatable dinghy
voyager par le train, prendre le train to travel by train *or* rail, take the train
être à *or* en vélo to be on a bike
venir à *or* en vélo to come by bike

* LES VÉHICULES

| | |
|---|---|
| une ambulance | ambulance |
| la bicyclette | bicycle |
| la camionnette | van |
| la caravane | caravan |
| la mobylette | moped |
| la moto, | |
| la motocyclette | motorbike, motorcycle |
| la voiture* | car |
| la voiture d'enfant | pram |
| la voiture de pompiers | fire engine |

**appelez l'ambulance!** call an ambulance!
**faire de la bicyclette** to go cycling
**aller à la ville en** *or* **à bicyclette** to go to town by bicycle, to cycle to town
**faire du caravaning** to go caravanning
**aller en voiture** to drive, go by car
**conduire (une voiture)** to (know how to) drive
**une promenade en voiture** a drive
**c'est à environ une heure de voiture de Londres** it's about an hour's drive from London
**la voiture de location** rented *or* hired car
**la voiture de sport** sports car
**la voiture de course** racing car
**la voiture décapotable** convertible

## ** LES VÉHICULES

| | |
|---|---|
| un **aérotrain** | hovertrain |
| le **bac*** | ferry(-boat) |
| le **bateau** (pl -x) à **rames/à voiles** | rowing/sailing boat |
| le **bateau-mouche** (pl **bateaux-mouches**) | bateau-mouche (*on the Seine*) |
| le **bulldozer** [buldozœr] | bulldozer |
| le **camion de déménagement** | removal van |
| le **canoë** [kanɔe] | canoe |
| le **canot automobile** | motorboat |
| le **canot de sauvetage** | lifeboat |
| le **car-ferry** | car ferry |
| le **funiculaire** | funicular (railway) |
| le **moyen de transport** | means of transport |
| le **paquebot** | passenger steamer, liner |
| le **semi-remorque** (pl **semi-remorques**) | articulated lorry |
| le **sous-marin** (pl **sous-marins**) | submarine |
| le **téléphérique** | cable-car |
| le **télésiège** | chairlift |
| le **tramway** | tram |
| le **vaisseau** (pl -x) | vessel |
| le **vapeur** | steamer |
| le **véhicule** | vehicle |
| le **yacht** [jɔt] | yacht |

**faire du bateau** to go sailing; to go boating
**faire du canoë** to go canoeing
**les transports en commun** public transport

## ** LES VÉHICULES

| | |
|---|---|
| la camionnette de livraison | delivery van |
| la charrette | cart |
| la fusée | rocket |
| la remorque | trailer |

**lancer une fusée/un navire** to launch a rocket/a ship
**partir comme une fusée** to shoot off like a rocket

*** LES VÉHICULES

| | |
|---|---|
| un aéroglisseur | hovercraft |
| un astronef | spaceship |
| le break [bʀɛk] | estate car |
| le camion-citerne (pl camions-citernes) | tanker |
| le char (d'assaut) | tank |
| le dirigeable | airship |
| l'hydravion | seaplane |
| le panier à salade | Black Maria |
| le pétrolier | oil tanker (ship) |
| le planeur | glider |
| le porte-avions (pl inv) | aircraft carrier |
| le remorqueur | tug, tugboat |

### *** LES VÉHICULES

| | |
|---|---|
| la jeep | jeep |
| la locomotive | engine, locomotive |
| la péniche | barge |
| la soucoupe volante | flying saucer |
| la vedette* | speedboat |
| la voiture pie | Panda car |

## * LES VÊTEMENTS

| | |
|---|---|
| un anorak | anorak |
| les bas | stockings |
| le béret | beret |
| le blue-jean [bludʒin] | |
| (pl bleu-jeans) | (pair of) jeans |
| le bouton* | button |
| le chapeau (pl -x) | hat |
| le complet | suit |
| le costume* | suit (for man); costume, dress |
| le gant | glove |
| un imperméable, un imper | raincoat |
| le jean* [dʒin] | (pair of) jeans |
| le maillot* (de bain) | swimsuit, swimming or bathing costume; trunks |
| le manteau (pl -x) | coat |
| le mouchoir | hankie, handkerchief |
| le pantalon | (pair of) trousers |
| le pardessus | overcoat |
| le pull-over [pylɔvɛr] | |
| (pl pull-overs), | sweater, jumper, |
| le pull | pullover |
| le pyjama | (pair of) pyjamas |
| le sac à main | handbag |
| le soulier | shoe |
| le tablier | apron |
| le veston | jacket (for man) |
| les vêtements | clothes |

**porter un béret/un pantalon** to wear a beret/trousers

**s'habiller** to get dressed, put on one's clothes

**se déshabiller** to get undressed, take off one's clothes

**se rhabiller** to get dressed again

**mettre son manteau/ses chaussures** to put on one's coat/one's shoes

**enlever** or **ôter son manteau/ses chaussures** to take off one's coat/one's shoes

**essayer** to try on; **se changer** to get changed

* LES VÊTEMENTS

| | |
|---|---|
| la blouse | smock, blouse |
| la botte, la bottine | boot |
| la canne* | cane, (walking) stick |
| la casquette | cap |
| la chaussette | sock |
| la chaussure | shoe |
| la chemise | shirt |
| la cravate | tie |
| une écharpe* | scarf |
| une espadrille | rope-soled sandal, espadrille |
| la jaquette | woman's jacket |
| la jupe | skirt |
| les lunettes | glasses |
| la mode | fashion |
| la poche* | pocket |
| la robe | dress |
| la veste | jacket (*for man or woman*); blazer |

à la mode in fashion
démodé old-fashioned
très chic very smart
cela vous va bien/mal that suits you/doesn't suit you
connaître une ville comme sa poche to know a town like the back of one's hand

## ** LES VÊTEMENTS

| | |
|---|---|
| les accessoires | accessories |
| le caleçon | (under)pants |
| le chandail | (thick) jumper |
| le chapeau (pl -x) melon | bowler hat |
| le chemisier | blouse |
| le col | collar |
| le col roulé | turtle neck |
| le collant | (pair of) tights |
| l'habit | evening dress, tails |
| en haillons | in rags |
| le képi | (military) cap |
| le lacet | (shoe)lace |
| le linge* | washing (*items to be washed*); underwear |
| le parapluie | umbrella |
| le pli | pleat |
| le short [ʃɔʀt] | (pair of) shorts |
| le slip | (under)pants |
| le slip de bain | swimming *or* bathing trunks |
| le soutien-gorge (pl soutiens-gorge) | bra, brassière |
| le tailleur* | woman's suit |
| les hauts talons | high heels |
| le T-shirt, le tee-shirt | T-shirt, tee-shirt |
| un uniforme | uniform |

**à plis** pleated
**en uniforme** in uniform
**en costume national** in national costume *or* dress

## ** LES VÊTEMENTS

| | |
|---|---|
| les bretelles | braces |
| la ceinture | belt |
| la chemise de nuit | nightie, nightdress |
| la fermeture éclair | zip |
| la:haute couture | haute couture |
| la pantoufle | slipper |
| la pointure | (shoe) size |
| la robe de chambre | dressing gown |
| la robe de mariée | wedding dress |
| la robe du soir | evening dress (*for woman*) |
| la sandale | sandal |
| la taille* | size; waist |

**fait sur mesure** made to measure
**le prêt-à-porter** ready-to-wear clothes
**acheter quelque chose en prêt-à-porter** to buy something off the peg
**prendre ses mesures** to measure oneself, take one's measurements
**la tour de taille/de poitrine** waist/chest *or* bust measurement
**tricoter, faire du tricot** to knit
**coudre, faire de la couture** to sew
**déchirer** to tear
**raccommoder** to mend
**se froisser** to get crushed *or* creased

**\*\*\* LES VÊTEMENTS**

| | |
|---|---|
| le bleu (or les bleus) de travail | overalls, dungarees |
| le blouson | bomber jacket |
| le duffel-coat [dœfœlkot] (pl duffel-coats) | duffel-coat |
| un ensemble pantalon | trouser suit |
| le foulard | scarf, headsquare |
| le gilet\* | waistcoat; cardigan |
| le gilet de corps or de peau | vest |
| le jupon | underskirt, petticoat |
| le nœud papillon | bow tie |
| le ruban | ribbon |
| le sac à bandoulière | shoulder bag |
| le survêtement | track suit |
| les talons aiguilles | stiletto heels |
| le tricot\* | jumper, jersey |
| le tricot de corps | vest |

les vêtements de détente or de loisir  casual clothes

### \*\*\* LES VÊTEMENTS

| | |
|---|---|
| la **boutonnière** | buttonhole |
| la **cabine d'essayage** | changing room |
| la **création** | model (*garment*) |
| la **culotte** | pants (*for child*) |
| la **manche** | sleeve |
| la **présentation de mode** | fashion show |
| la **salopette** | dungarees; overalls |
| les **semelles compensées** | platform soles |

**porter une fleur à sa boutonnière** to wear a flower in one's buttonhole

**en tenue du soir** in evening dress (*man or woman*)

**en bras de chemise** in one's shirt sleeves

**à manches courtes/longues** short-sleeved/long-sleeved

* LA VILLE

| | |
|---|---|
| un **agent (de police)** | policeman |
| un **arrêt (de bus)** | bus stop |
| le **boulevard** | avenue, boulevard |
| le **bureau** *(pl -x)* **de poste** | post office |
| le **camion** | lorry, truck |
| le **carnet de tickets** | book of tickets |
| le **centre-ville** | the town centre |
| le **château** *(pl -x)* | castle |
| le **cinéma** | cinema |
| le **coin** | corner |
| un **embouteillage** | traffic jam |
| les **environs** | the surroundings, the outskirts |
| l'**habitant** | inhabitant |
| l'**hôpital** *(pl hôpitaux)* | hospital |
| l'**hôtel\*** | hotel; mansion |
| un **(grand) immeuble** | block of flats |
| le **jardin public** | public park |
| le **jour de marché** | market day |
| le **journal** *(pl journaux)* | newspaper |
| le **kiosque (à journaux)** | (newspaper) stall |
| le **magasin** | shop |
| le **maire** | mayor |
| le **marché\*** | market |
| le **métro** | underground |
| le **monument** | monument |
| le **musée** | museum |
| le **panneau** *(pl -x)* | roadsign |
| le **parking** | car park |
| le **passage clouté** | pedestrian crossing |
| le **passant** | passer-by |
| le **piéton** | pedestrian |
| le **restaurant** | restaurant |
| le **taxi** | taxi |
| le **théâtre** | theatre |
| le **trottoir** | pavement |

**en ville** in town
**aller en ville** to go into town

**\* LA VILLE**

| | |
|---|---|
| une affiche | notice; poster |
| une auto | car |
| la cathédrale | cathedral |
| la chaussée | roadway |
| la circulation | traffic |
| une église | church |
| la fabrique | factory |
| la foule | crowd |
| la gare | (train) station |
| la grand'route | main road |
| la grand-rue | main street |
| la mairie | town hall |
| la place\* | square |
| la police | police |
| la pollution de l'air | air pollution |
| la population | population |
| la poste\* | post office |
| la queue\* [kø] | queue |
| la route | road |
| la rue | street |
| la rue principale | main street |
| la station-service | service station, garage |
| la tour | tower |
| une usine | factory |
| la ville | town, city |
| la voiture\* | car |
| la voiture d'enfant | pram |

une rue à sens unique  a one-way street
traverser la rue  to cross the street

**\*\* LA VILLE**

| | |
|---|---|
| un **arrondissement** | district |
| le **bâtiment** | building |
| le **bistrot** | café |
| le **carrefour** | crossroads |
| le **citoyen** | citizen |
| le **commissariat de police** | police station |
| le **défilé** | procession, parade |
| le **gratte-ciel** *(pl inv)* | skyscraper |
| l'**hôtel de ville** | town hall |
| le **quartier** | district |
| les **signaux routiers** | roadsigns |
| le **stationnement** | parking |
| le **syndicat d'initiative** | tourist information office |
| le **tour\*** | tour |
| le **véhicule** | vehicle |

**\*\*\* LA VILLE**

| | |
|---|---|
| un **abribus** | bus shelter |
| un **autobus à impériale/sans impériale** | double/single decker bus |
| le **cimetière** | cemetery, graveyard |
| le **citadin** | town dweller |
| le **comté** | county |
| le **conseil municipal** | town council |
| le **département** | *same as British 'region'* |
| un **édifice** | building |
| un **égout** | sewer |
| le **faubourg** | suburb |
| le **pavé** | cobblestone; paving stone |
| le **refuge** | traffic island |
| le **réverbère** | street lamp |
| le **sondage d'opinion** | opinion poll |
| le **square** | square with gardens |
| le **tournant**, le **virage** | turning, bend |

## ** LA VILLE

| | |
|---|---|
| une agglomération | built-up area |
| la banlieue | suburbs |
| la bousculade | bustle, crush |
| la boutique | (small) shop |
| la camionnette de livraison | delivery van |
| la caserne de pompiers | fire station |
| la cité | city (*old part*) |
| la flèche* | spire; arrow |
| la galerie d'art | art gallery |
| la gare routière | coach station |
| une H.L.M. (habitation à loyer modéré) | council flat |
| la prison | prison |
| la station de taxis | taxi rank |
| la statue | statue |

## *** LA VILLE

| | |
|---|---|
| la cité universitaire | university halls of residence |
| les curiosités | the sights, the places of interest |
| une impasse | dead end |
| la piste cyclable | cycle path |

**visiter la ville** to go sightseeing (*in town*)

The vocabulary items on pages 206 to 236 have been grouped under parts of speech rather than themes because they can apply in a wide range of circumstances. Please use them just as freely as the nouns already given.

# LES CONJONCTIONS

## LES CONJONCTIONS

**alors que** when
**aussi** so, therefore
**aussi . . . que** as . . . as
**avant de** + *infinitive* before
**car** for
**cependant** however
**c'est-à-dire** that is to say
**comme** as
**comment** how
**depuis que** since
**dès que** as soon as
**donc** so, then
**et** and
**lorsque** when
**maintenant que** now (that)
**mais** but

**au moment où** just as
**ni . . . ni** neither . . . nor
**or** now
**ou** or
**parce que** because
**pendant que** while
**pourquoi** why
**pourvu que** + *subj* provided that, as long as
**puis** then
**puisque** since, because
**quand** when
**que** that; than
**si** if
**sinon** otherwise
**tandis que** whilst
**tant que** so long as, while
**vu que** seeing (that)

## LES ADJECTIFS

**abordable** within reach
**abrégé(e)** shortened
**absurde** absurd
**actif, active** active
**actuel(le)** present (*time*)
**aérien(ne)** aerial
**affectueux, -euse** affectionate
**affreux, -euse** frightful
**âgé(e)** old
**agité** restless; busy (*street*); stormy (*sea*)
**agréable** pleasant
**agricole** agricultural
**aigu, aiguë** acute; piercing
**aimable** kind, nice
**aîné(e)** elder, eldest
**amer, amère** bitter
**amusant(e)** amusing, enjoyable
**ancien(ne)** old, former
**animé(e)** busy, crowded
**annuel(le)** annual
**anonyme** anonymous
**anormal(e)** abnormal
**anxieux, -ieuse** anxious, worried
**appliqué(e)** diligent
**apte** capable
**arrière: siège m arrière** back seat
**assis(e)** sitting, seated
**aucun(e)** any, no, not any
**automatique** automatic
**autre** other
**avant: siège m avant** front seat

**barbu** bearded
**bas(se)** low
**beau (bel), belle** beautiful, fine
**bête** silly
**bien** well
**bienvenu(e)** welcome
**bizarre** strange, odd
**blessé(e)** injured
**bon(ne)** good
**bordé(e) de** lined with
**bouillant(e)** boiling
**bouleversé(e)** thrown into confusion
**brave** fine, good
**bref, brève** brief
**brillant(e)** bright, brilliant; shiny
**brutal(e)** brutal
**bruyant(e)** noisy
**calme** calm
**capable** capable
**carré(e)** square
**célèbre** famous
**certain(e)** sure, certain
**chaque** each, every
**chargé(e) de** loaded with
**charmant(e)** delightful
**chaud(e)** warm; hot
**cher, chère** dear
**chic** smart
**choquant(e)** shocking
**civil(e)** civil
**clair(e)** clear; light
**classique** classical
**climatisé(e)** air-conditioned
**commode** convenient;

handy
**complet, complète**
complete
**compliqué(e)**
complicated
**composé(e) de**
comprising
**confortable** comfortable
**contemporain(e)**
contemporary
**content(e)** happy
**continuel(le)** continuing
**convenable** suitable
**couché(e)** lying down
**courageux, -euse**
courageous
**court(e)** short
**couvert(e) de** covered
with
**créé(e)** created,
established
**cruel(le)** cruel
**cuit(e)** cooked
**culturel(le)** cultural
**curieux, -ieuse** curious,
strange
**dangereux, -euse**
dangerous
**debout** standing (up)
**décevant(e)** disappoint-
ing
**découragé(e)** discouraged
**déçu(e)** disappointed
**dégoûté(e)** disgusted
**délabré(e)** dilapidated
**délicat(e)** delicate
**délicieux, -ieuse**
delicious
**dernier, dernière** last,
latest

**désagréable** unpleasant
**désert(e)** deserted
**désespéré(e)** desperate
**détestable** foul, ghastly
**détruit(e)** destroyed
**différent(e)** different
**difficile** difficult
**digne** worthy
**distingué(e)**
distinguished
**distrait(e)** absent-
minded
**divers(e)** different
**divertissant(e)**
entertaining
**divin(e)** divine
**divisé(e)** divided
**doré(e)** golden; gilt
**doux, douce** gentle;
sweet; soft
**droit(e)** straight;
right(hand)
**drôle** funny
**dur(e)** hard
**éclairé(e): bien éclairé(e)**
well lit
**effrayé(e)** frightened
**élaboré(e)** elaborate
**électrique** electric
**élémentaire** elementary
**élevé(e)** high
**embêtant(e)** annoying
**émouvant** moving
**enchanté(e)** delighted
**enfantin(e)** childlike;
childish
**ennuyé(e)** bothered;
annoyed
**ennuyeux, -euse** boring
**énorme** huge

entier, entière whole
épais, épaisse thick
épouvantable terrible
épuisé(e) exhausted, worn out
étendu(e) stretched out
étonnant(e) astonishing
étonné(e) astonished
d'un air étonné in astonishment
étrange strange
étranger, étrangère foreign
étroit(e) narrow; strict
éveillé(e) awake
évident(e) evident, obvious
exact(e) exact
excellent(e) excellent
exclusif, -ive exclusive
expérimenté(e) experienced
exquis(e) exquisite
extraordinaire extraordinary
fâché(e) angry
facile easy
fatigant(e) tiring
fatigué(e) tired
faux, fausse false, wrong
favori(te) favourite
ferme firm
féroce fierce
fier, fière proud
fin(e) fine; thin
final(e) final
fondé(e) founded
formidable tremendous, magnificent
fort(e) strong; hard

fortuné(e) fortunate
fou, folle mad
un succès fou a great success
frais, fraîche fresh, cool
frappant(e) striking
frêle frail
froid(e) cold
furieux, -ieuse furious
futur(e) future
gai(e) gay
garni(e) garnished
gauche left(hand)
général(e) general
gentil(le) kind, nice
gonflé(e) blown up
gracieux, -euse graceful
grand(e) big, great; tall; high
gratuit(e) free
grave serious
grêle slender
gros(se) big; fat
habile skilful
habitué(e) accustomed
habitué(e) à used to
habituel(le) usual
haut(e) high
heureux, -euse happy
hideux, -euse hideous
historique historic(al)
honnête honest
humoristique humorous
identique identical
illuminé(e) floodlit
illustré(e) illustrated
imaginaire imaginary
immense huge, immense

impénitent(e) unrepentant
important(e) important
impossible impossible
impressionnant(e) impressive
impressionniste impressionist
imprévu(e) unforeseen
inattendu(e) unexpected
incapable (de) incapable (of)
inconnu(e) unknown
incroyable unbelievable
indispensable indispensable
industriel(le) industrial
inondé(e) flooded
inquiet, inquiète anxious, worried
insouciant(e) carefree
insupportable horrid, unbearable
intact(e) intact
intelligent(e) intelligent
interdit(e) prohibited
intéressant(e) interesting
interminable endless
interrompu(e) interrupted
inutile useless
irrité(e) annoyed
isolé(e) isolated
jaloux, -ouse jealous
jeune young
joli(e) pretty
joyeux, -euse merry, cheerful

juste just; correct
lâche cowardly
laid(e) ugly
large wide
léger, légère light
lent(e) slow
libre free, vacant
local(e) local
long(ue) long
lourd(e) heavy
de luxe luxurious, luxury
magnifique magnificent
maigre thin
malade ill
malheureux, -euse unhappy, unfortunate
marqué(e) (de) marked (with)
masqué(e) masked
mauvais(e) bad
à la mauvaise ligne on the wrong line
de mauvaise humeur in a bad temper
mécanique mechanical
méchant(e) naughty, bad
méconnu(e) unrecognized
mécontent(e) unhappy
médical(e) medical
meilleur(e) better, best
même same
menu(e) tiny
merveilleux, -euse marvellous
militaire military
minable pathetic, pitiful
mince slim, slender
moderne modern
moindre least

montagneux, -euse mountainous

mort(e) dead

mouillé(e) wet through

mouvementé(e) lively

moyen(ne) average

mû, mue (par) moved (by)

multicolore multicoloured

muni(e) de provided with

municipal(e) municipal, town

mûr(e) ripe

musclé(e) muscular, brawny

musical(e) musical

mystérieux, -euse mysterious

natal(e) native

national(e) national

né(e) born

nécessaire necessary

nerveux, -euse nervous

net(te) clear, sharp

neuf, neuve new

nombreux, -euse numerous

nommé(e) called, named

nouveau (nouvel), nouvelle new

noyé(e) drowned

nul: match nul match drawn

obligatoire compulsory

obligé(e): être obligé(e) de to be obliged to

occupé(e) engaged, taken (of room); busy (of person)

officiel(le) official

ombreux, -euse shady, dim

ordinaire ordinary

original(e) original

orné(e) de decorated with

outré(e) outraged, appalled

pâle pale

pareil(le) similar, same une somme pareille such a sum

paresseux, -euse lazy

parfait(e) perfect

particulier, particulière particular; private

passionnant(e) exciting

passionné(e) passionate

patient(e) patient

pauvre poor

pénible painful

perpétuel(le) perpetual

personnel(le) personal

petit(e) small, little

plat(e) flat

plein(e) (de) full (of)

en plein air in the open air

en plein jour in broad daylight

plusieurs several

pneumatique inflatable

poli(e) polite; polished

populaire popular

portatif, -ive portable

possible possible

poudreux, -euse powdery

pratique practical

précis(e) precise

à cinq heures précises at

exactly five o'clock
**préfabriqué(e)**
prefabricated
**préféré(e)** favourite
**préliminaire**
preliminary
**premier, première** first
**présentable** presentable
**pressant(e)** urgent
**pressé(e): être pressé(e)**
to be in a hurry
**prêt(e)** ready
**prêt à porter** ready to
wear, off-the-peg
**primaire** primary
**privilégié(e)** privileged
**prochain(e)** next
**proche** nearby; close
**profond(e)** deep
**propre** own; clean
**prudent(e)** cautious
**public, publique** public
**publicitaire** publicity
**quel(le)** what
**quelque** some
**rafraîchissant(e)**
refreshing
**rangé(e): bien rangé(e)**
neat and tidy
**rapide** fast, quick, rapid
**rare** rare
**rauque** harsh
**ravi(e)** delighted
**récent(e)** recent
**reconnaissant(e)**
grateful
**religieux, -ieuse**
religious
**reluisant(e)** shining
**réservé(e)** reserved

**responsable (de)**
responsible (for)
**rêveur, -euse** dreamy
**riche** rich
**ridicule** ridiculous
**romantique** romantic
**rond(e)** round
**roulé(e)** rolled up
**rusé(e)** cunning
**sage** good, well-behaved;
wise
**sain et sauf** safe and
sound
**sale** dirty
**un sale temps** terrible
weather
**sanitaire** sanitary
**satisfait(e) (de)** satisfied
(with)
**sauvage** uncivilized; wild
**scolaire** school (year etc)
**sec, sèche** dry
**second(e)** second
**secondaire** secondary
**secret, secrète** secret
**sensationnel(le)**
sensational
**sérieux, -ieuse** serious
**serré(e)** tight, close
**seul(e)** alone; single
**sévère** severe, strict
**simple** simple, plain
**sincère** sincere
**sinistre** sinister
**situé(e)** situated
**solennel(le)** solemn
**sombre** dark
**peu soucieux (soucieuse)**
unconcerned
**soupçonneux, -euse**

suspicious
souriant(e) smiling
sous-marin(e) underwater
spécial(e) special
suivi(e) de followed by
superbe magnificent
supérieur(e) advanced
supplémentaire extra
supportable bearable
sûr(e) sure
surnommé(e) nicknamed
sympathique likeable; attractive; kind
taciturne uncommunicative
technique technical
tel(le) such
terrible terrible
théâtral(e) theatrical
timide shy
touristique touristic
tout(e) all
traditionnel(le) traditional
tranquille quiet, peaceful

trempé soaked
trente-six umpteen
triste sad
troublé(e) worried, disturbed
typique typical
uni(e) plain
unique only (hope etc); unique
urbain(e) urban
urgent(e) urgent
utile useful
varié(e) varied; various
vaste vast
véritable real, genuine
vide empty
vieux (vieil), vieille old
vif, vive keen; vivid
un vif plaisir great pleasure
vilain(e) wretched, naughty; ugly
vinicole wine-growing
violent(e) violent
vivant(e) alive, lively
voisin(e) neighbouring
vrai(e) real, true

## LES ADVERBES ET LES PRÉPOSITIONS

**à** to, at
**d'abord** first, at first
**tout d'abord** first of all
**aux abords de** alongside
**absolument** absolutely
**actuellement** at present
**admirablement**
admirably
**afin de** so as to
**ailleurs** elsewhere
**d'ailleurs** moreover
**ainsi** thus
**ainsi que** as well as
**en plein air** in the open
air
**d'un air étonné** in
astonishment
**alors** then; so
**anxieusement** anxiously
**après** after
**après-demain** the day
after tomorrow
**d'après** according to
**assez** fairly, quite
**assez de** enough
**à l'attention de** for the
attention of
**aujourd'hui** today
**auparavant** previously
**auprès de** by, close to,
next to
**aussi** also, too
**aussitôt** at once
**autant (de)** as much; as
many
**d'autant plus de** all the
more
**en automne** in autumn

**autour de** around
**autrefois** formerly
**autrement** otherwise,
differently
**autrement que** other
than
**à l'avance** in advance
**avant (de)** before
**avec** with
**à mon avis** in my opinion
**en bas** downstairs, at the
bottom
**beaucoup** very much,
many
**beaucoup de** a lot of
**bien** well
**bien entendu** of course
**bientôt** soon
**à bord (de)** on board
**au bord de** beside
**au bout de** after (*of time*);
at the end of
**bref** 'to cut a long story
short'
**brusquement** abruptly,
sharply
**à la campagne** in the
country
**en cas de** in the case of
**en tout cas** in any case
**à cause de** because of
**par centaines** in
hundreds
**certainement** certainly
**sans cesse** without
stopping, unceasingly
**chez** at (*or* to) the house
of

**en colère (contre)** angry (with)
**combien (de)** how much, how many
**comme** as, like
**comme d'habitude** as usual
**comme toujours** as usual
**comment?** how?
**complètement** completely
**y compris** including
**par conséquent** as a result
**continuellement** continually
**au contraire** on the contrary
**contre** against
**ci-contre** opposite (this)
**par contre** on the other hand
**à côté de** next to, beside
**de ce côté (de)** on this side (of)
**de l'autre côté (de)** on the other side (of)
**juste à côté** next door
**au cours de** during, in the course of
**en cours** in progress
**dans** in
**davantage (de)** more
**de** of, from
**debout** standing
**dedans** inside
**(au) dehors** outside
**déjà** already
**demain** tomorrow
**après-demain** the day after tomorrow

**depuis** since, for
**depuis lors** since then
**derrière** behind
**dès** from (time)
**ci-dessous** below (this)
**au-dessus de** above
**ci-dessus** above (this)
**devant** in front (of)
**doucement** quietly, gently
**sans doute** no doubt
**tout droit** straight (on)
**à droite** on the right, to the right
**dur: travailler dur** to work hard
**en échange de** in exchange for
**en effet** in effect; as a matter of fact, in fact
**également** also, equally
**à cet égard** in this respect
**encore** still; again
**encore une fois** once again
**enfin** finally, at last
**sans engagement** without obligation
**énormément (de)** a lot (of)
**ensemble** together
**ensuite** then, next
**entièrement** entirely
**entre** between
**environ** about
**en espèces** in cash
**au premier étage** on the first floor
**en été** in summer

**à l'étranger** abroad
**évidemment** evidently, obviously
**exactement** exactly
**par exemple** for example
**exprès** on purpose, deliberately
**à l'extérieur (de)** outside
**extrêmement** extremely
**face à** facing
**en face (de)** opposite
**facilement** easily
**de façon à** so as to
**d'une façon sauvage** wildly
**en famille** with the family; as a family
**fidèlement** faithfully
**une fois** once
**une fois de plus** once more
**à la fois** at the same time
**encore une fois** once again
**au fond de** at the bottom of, at the far end of
**fort: pleuvoir fort** to rain hard
**à gauche** on the left, to the left
**en général** usually
**généralement** generally
**gentiment** nicely
**grâce à** thanks to
**pas grand-chose** not much
**ne . . . guère** hardly
**d'habitude** usually
**comme d'habitude** as usual

**par hasard** by chance
**au hasard** at random
**en haut (de)** at the top (of)
**de haut en bas** from top to bottom
**à l'heure** on time
**tout à l'heure** (*recent past*) a short while ago, just now; (*near future*) in a little while, shortly
**de bonne heure** early
**heureusement** fortunately
**hier** yesterday
**avant-hier** the day before yesterday
**en hiver** in winter
**ici** here
**en imagination** in (one's) mind
**immédiatement** immediately
**n'importe où** anywhere
**intellectuellement** intellectually
**à l'intérieur (de)** inside
**jadis** formerly, once
**jamais** ever
**ne . . . jamais** never
**en plein jour** in broad daylight
**par jour** daily
**de nos jours** these days, nowadays
**jusqu'à** until, as far as, up to
**jusqu'ici** so far, until now
**jusque-là** until then

**justement** exactly
**là** there
**là-bas** over there, down there
**là-haut** up there
**légèrement** slightly; lightly
**le lendemain** the next day
**le lendemain matin** the next morning
**lentement** slowly
**lieu: au lieu de** instead of, in place of
**au lit** in bed
**loin (de)** far (from), a long way (from)
**le long de** along
**longtemps** (for) a long time
**lourdement** heavily
**depuis lors** since then
**maintenant** now
**à la maison** at home
**mal** badly
**malgré** in spite of, despite
**malheureusement** unfortunately
**manuellement** manually
**au maximum** at (the) most, to the utmost
**même** same; even
**même pas** not even
**quand même** even so
**mentalement** mentally
**(fait) sur mesure** made to measure
**mieux** better
**le mieux** best
**au milieu de** in the

middle of
**à la mode** in fashion
**moins** less, minus
**moins de** less than, fewer than
**au moins** at least (quantity)
**du moins** at least
**en ce moment** at the moment
**à ce moment-là** at that very moment
**sans mot dire** without saying a word
**au moyen de** by means of
**mystérieusement** mysteriously
**naturellement** of course, naturally
**au négatif** in the negative
**nerveusement** nervously
**normalement** normally
**notamment** especially
**de nouveau** again
**nulle part** nowhere
**ne . . . nullement** in no way
**à l'ombre (de)** in the shade (of)
**en ordre** in order
**où** where
**n'importe où** anywhere
**en outre** furthermore
**en paix** in peace
**par** by; through
**par terre** on the ground
**par-dessus** over
**parfois** sometimes
**parmi** among
**à part** apart (from)

**de ma part** on my behalf
**nulle part** nowhere
**quelque part** somewhere
**en particulier** in particular
**particulièrement** particularly
**partiellement** partially
**à partir de** from
**partout** everywhere
**pas du tout** not at all
**pas loin de** not far from
**patiemment** patiently
**à peine** scarcely, hardly, barely
**pendant** during, for
**peu à peu** little by little
**à peu près** about, approximately
**peut-être** perhaps, maybe
**à pied** on foot
**poliment** politely
**au premier plan** in the foreground
**à l'arrière-plan** in the background
**en plein jour** in broad daylight
**plus** [plys] plus
**en plus** [plys] moreover
**plus de (pommes)** [ply] no more (apples)
**plus de (dix)** [ply] more than (ten)
**de plus** [plys] moreover
**de plus en plus** [dəplyzã-ply] more and more
**ne . . . plus** [ply] no more, no longer

**plus tard** [ply] later
**non plus** [ply] neither, either
**moi non plus!** nor me!
**plutôt** rather
**à portée de la main** within reach
**pour** for; in order to
**pourtant** yet, nevertheless
**près de** near (to)
**à présent** at present
**presque** almost, nearly
**en proie à** as a prey to
**au printemps** in spring
**à proximité de** near to
**avec prudence** carefully
**puis** then, next
**quand** when
**quand même** however, even so, nevertheless
**quant à (moi)** as for (me)
**quelquefois** sometimes
**quelque part** somewhere
**au premier rang** in the forefront; in the first row
**rarement** rarely, seldom
**récemment** recently
**sous le règne de** in the reign of
**régulièrement** regularly
**en retard** late
**en retour de** in return for
**en retraite de** away from
**sans risque** safely
**en route pour** on the way to
**sans** without
**sans cesse** without stopping, ceaselessly

**sans doute** no doubt
**sauf** except (for)
**en scène** on stage
**selon** according to
**sérieusement** seriously
**de service** on duty
**seulement** only
**simplement** simply
**soigneusement** carefully
**avec soin** carefully
**soit!** all right!, so be it!
**soudain** suddenly
**sous** under
**souvent** often
**suite** 'continued'
**à la suite de** following
**suivant** according to, following
**suivi(e) de** followed by
**à suivre** to be continued
**au sujet de** about, concerning
**sur** on
**bien sûr** of course
**sûrement** certainly, surely
**sur-le-champ** at once
**surtout** especially
**tant de** so much, so many
**tard** late
**plus tard** later
**trop tard** too late
**tellement** so, very much
**à temps** in time
**de temps en temps** now and then, from time to time
**de temps à autre** from time to time
**en même temps** at the same time
**par terre** on the ground
**tôt** early
**trop tôt** too soon, too early
**le plus tôt possible** as soon as possible
**toujours** always; still
**en tout** in all
**tout d'abord** first of all
**tout à coup** suddenly
**tout à fait** completely, quite
**tout à l'heure** (*recent past*) a short while ago, just now; (*near future*) in a little while, shortly
**tout près (de)** quite close (to)
**tout de suite** at once
**à toute vitesse** at full or top speed
**tous les deux, toutes les deux** both
**à travers** through
**très** very
**trop** too
**trop de** too much, too many
**un à un** one by one
**en vain** in vain
**vers** towards, about (*of time*)
**en ville** to town, in town
**vite** quickly
**de vue** by sight
**en vue de** in view of
**y** there, to that place, in that place

## ENCORE DES NOMS!

un accord* agreement
un accueil m reception
l'action f action
l'activité f activity
l'âge f age
l'ambition f ambition
l'âme f soul
l'amour m love
l'angoisse f anguish, distress
une annonce advertisement
l'arrière m back, rear
l'attention f attention; see faire
un attrait attraction
un avantage advantage
une aventure adventure
un avis notice; opinion
à mon avis in my opinion
la bataille battle
le bâton stick
la beauté beauty
le besoin see avoir
la bêtise stupidity
le bien good
le bonheur happiness, good luck
la bousculade bustle
le bout end
le bruit noise
le but* aim; goal
le calme peace, calm
le candidat candidate
le caractère character, nature
la catastrophe disaster
le centre centre

le cercle circle
le chagrin distress
la chance luck
le chapitre chapter
le chef* chief, head, boss
le choix choice
la chose thing
le chuchotement whispering
la civilisation civilization
le classement classification
le clocher steeple
le coin corner
la colère anger; see mettre
la colonne column
le commencement beginning
la comparaison comparison; see soutenir
le compte calculation
la confiance confidence
le confort comfort
la connaissance see faire
la conscience conscience
le conseil (piece of) advice
la construction construction
la copie copy
la corbeille basket
le/la correspondant(e) correspondent
le coup blow, bang, knock
le courage courage, bravery

la **coutume** custom
la **crainte** fear
le **cri** cry
la **culture\*** culture
la **curiosité** curiosity
le **danger** danger
les **débris** wreckage
le **début** beginning
la **décision** decision
les **dégâts** damage
le **désastre** disaster
le **désir** desire, wish
le **désordre** disorder
le **destin** destiny
le **détail** detail
la **détresse** distress
la **déveine** bad luck
le (bon) **Dieu** God
la **différence** difference
quelle est la **différence**
entre X et Y? what is the
difference between X and
Y?
la **difficulté** difficulty
le **désavantage** disadvantage
la **dimension** dimension
la **direction** direction
la **discipline** discipline
la **dispute** argument, dispute
la **distance** distance
le **droit** right
la **durée** time
l'**économie** f economy
un **effet** effect
un **effort** effort
un **électeur** elector
une **élection** election
l'**élégance** f elegance

un **endroit** place
l'**énergie** f energy
l'**ennemi** m enemy
l'**ennui** m annoyance,
boredom
une **enseigne** sign
un **ensemble** group (of
buildings etc)
l'**enthousiasme** m
enthusiasm
un **entretien** conversation, discussion
**envie** see avoir
les **environs** mpl sur-
rounding district
l'**épaisseur** f thickness
une **erreur** mistake
l'**espace** f space
une **espèce** sort, kind,
species
un **espoir** hope
l'**essentiel** m the main
thing
une **étape** stage
un **état** state
l'**étendue** f extent
l'**étonnement** m
astonishment
un **événement** event
un **excès** excess
un **exemple** example
l'**exil** m exile
l'**expérience** f experience
un **expert** expert
une **explication**
explanation
une **exposition**
exhibition
un **extrait** extract
la **fabrication**

manufacture

la façon way, method, manner

de cette façon in this way

le fait fact

la faute* fault

c'est de ma faute it's my fault

la fermeture closure

la fin end

la flèche* arrow

la foi faith

la fois time

la folie madness

la forme form, shape

le fond background; bottom

la foule crowd

la fraîcheur freshness

les frais expenses

le franc franc

la gaieté, la gaîté gaiety

le genre type, kind, sort

la gentillesse kindness

les goûts interests

chacun son goût every man to his taste

le gouvernement government

la grandeur size

le gros lot first prize (in lottery)

le groupe group

la guerre war

le guide guide

l'habileté f skill

l'habitude see avoir

le:haut-parleur (pl haut-parleurs) loudspeaker

la:hauteur height

l'honneur m honour

les honoraires mpl fees

la:honte shame

la:humeur humour, mood

l'hygiène f hygiene

une idée idea

un/une idiot(e) idiot

une image picture

l'imagination f imagination

un/une imbécile idiot, imbecile

l'inconvénient m disadvantage

l'importance f importance

une impression impression

un/une inconnu(e) stranger

un inconvénient disadvantage

les informations fpl information; news

un inspecteur inspector

les instructions fpl instructions

l'intention f see avoir

l'intérêt m interest

une interruption break, interruption

une interview interview

la jalousie jealousy, envy

la joie joy

le jouet toy

le journal (pl journaux) newspaper

la largeur width

la larme tear
le lecteur reader
la légende caption
le lieu place; *see* avoir
la ligne line
la limite boundary, limit
la liste list
la littérature literature
le livre (sterling) pound (sterling)
les locaux premises
le loisir leisure
la longueur length
la Loterie Nationale National Lottery
la lumière light
la machine machine
le magazine magazine
la malchance bad luck
le malheur misfortune
la manière way, method
le manque (de) lack (of)
le maximum maximum
le mélange mixture
le membre member
la mémoire memory
la méthode method, way
le mieux best; *see* faire
le milieu centre, middle
le minimum minimum
le Ministère de the Ministry of
la morale morals
le mot word; note, message
le moyen (de) the means (of)
le mystère mystery
le niveau (*pl* -x) level
le nombre number

la nouvelle news
une objection objection
un objet object
une observation remark
une occasion chance
les odeurs *mpl* fumes; smell
les œuvres *fpl* works
un ordre order
l'orgueil *m* pride
l'ouverture *f* opening
la page page
la paire pair
le panier basket
le panneau (*pl* -x) sign, notice
le pari bet
la parole word
la partie* part; *see* faire
le pas footstep
la patience patience
la peine difficulty
la pensée* thought
la permission permission
la personne person
la phrase sentence
la pièce (de 10 centimes) 10-centime coin
la plaisanterie joke
le plaisir pleasure
le plan plan, map
la plupart de *or* des most (of)
le poids weight
le point point, mark
le point de départ starting point
le point de vue point of view

la **politesse** politeness
la **politique** politics
le **portrait** portrait
la **position** position
la **possibilité** possibility, opportunity
la **poupée** doll
le **pouvoir** power
les **préparatifs** *mpl* preparations
la **préparation** preparation
la **présence** presence
le **pressentiment** feeling
le **problème** problem
le **produit** product; produce
la **profondeur** depth
le **projet** plan
la **propreté** cleanliness
la **prospérité** prosperity
les **provisions** provisions
la **publicité** publicity
la **qualité** quality
la **question** question
le **raccourci** short-cut
la **raison** reason; *see* avoir
le **rapport** connection
la **religion** religion
les **remerciements** *mpl* thanks
le **remue-ménage** stir, hullaballoo
la **rencontre*** meeting
le **rendez-vous** appointment; meeting place
les **renseignements** *mpl* information
la **réponse** reply
la **reprise** resumption

la **réputation** reputation
le **rescapé** survivor
le **réseau** (*pl* -x) network
la **résolution** resolution
le **respect** respect
les **restes** *mpl* remains
le **résultat** result
le **retour** return
la **réussite** success
la **révolution** revolution
le **révolutionnaire** revolutionary
le **rythme** rhythm
la **saleté** dirtiness
le **sang-froid** calmness
le **sanglot** sob
le **schéma** diagram, plan
le **secours** help
le **secret** secret
la **section** section
la **sécurité** security
le **séjour** stay
la **sélection** selection
le **sens** sense
la **série** series
le **service** service
le **signe** sign
le **silence** silence
le **sinistre** disaster
la **situation** situation
la **société** society
la **solution** solution
la **somme** sum
le **son** sound
le **sort** fate
la **sorte** sort, kind
le **soupçon** suspicion
le **sourire** smile
le **souvenir** souvenir
le **spectateur** spectator

14

le **style** style
le **succès** success
la **surprise** surprise
la **surveillance** supervision; watch
le **système** system
la **tâche** task
le **talent** talent
le **taux de change** exchange rate
la **taxe** tax
la **tentative** attempt
le **terme** term, expression
le **texte** text
la **timidité** shyness
le **tour*** turn; trick
**c'est ton tour** it's your turn

le **tournoi** tournament
la **trace** sign, trace
la **tristesse** sadness
le **tube** tube
le **type** fellow, chap, sort, kind
le **va-et-vient** coming and going
la **valeur** value
la **veine*** luck
la **version** version
le **verso** back (of page)
la **victoire** victory
la **vie** life
les **vœux** *mpl* wishes
le **voyage** journey

## LES VERBES

**abandonner** to abandon
**aboutir** to end
**s'abriter** to shelter
**accepter** to accept
**accompagner** to go with
**accomplir** to accomplish
**s'accoutumer à** to become accustomed to
**accrocher** to hang (up); to catch (à on)
**accueillir** to welcome
**achever** to finish
**acquitter** to endorse
**admettre** to admit
**adorer** to adore
**s'adresser à** to apply to; to speak to
**affecter (de faire quelque chose)** to pretend (to do something)
**afficher** to display
**affirmer** to maintain, assert
**agacer** to irritate, aggravate
**agir** to act, behave
**il s'agit de** it is a question of
**agiter le bras** to wave
**s'agrandir** to grow
**aider quelqu'un à** to help somebody
**aimer** to like, love
**ajouter** to add
**aller** to go
**aller chercher quelqu'un** to fetch somebody, go and meet somebody

**s'en aller** to go away
**allumer** to switch on; to light
**amarrer** to moor
**s'amuser** to enjoy oneself
**annoncer** to announce
**s'apercevoir de** to notice
**appartenir (à)** to belong (to)
**appeler** to call
**s'appeler** to be called
**apporter** to bring
**apprécier** to appreciate
**apprendre (à faire)** to learn (to do)
**apprendre quelque chose à quelqu'un** to teach somebody something
**(s')approcher de** to approach
**appuyer** to press; to lean (object)
**s'appuyer** to lean
**arracher** to pull out; to snatch; to tear
**s'arranger: cela s'arrangera** it will be all right
**arrêter** to stop; to arrest
**s'arrêter** to stop
**arriver** to arrive; to happen
**s'asseoir** to sit down
**assister à** to attend, be present at, go to
**assurer** to assure; to ensure
**attacher** to tie, fasten
**attaquer** to attack

**atteindre** to reach
**attendre** to wait (for); to expect
**attirer** to attract
**attraper** to catch
**augmenter** to increase
**(s')avancer** to go forward
**avoir** to have
**avoir l'air (de)** to seem (to)
**avoir besoin de** to need
**avoir envie de** to want to
**avoir l'habitude de** to be in the habit of
**avoir honte (de)** to be ashamed (of)
**avoir l'intention de** to intend to
**avoir lieu** to take place, to occur
**avoir du mal à** to have difficulty in
**avoir peur** to be afraid
**avoir raison/tort** to be right/wrong
**avouer** to confess
**baisser** to lower
**balbutier** to stammer
**barrer** to block
**bâtir** to build
**battre** to beat
**se battre** to fight
**bavarder** to gossip, chat
**bloquer** to block
**bouger** to move
**bouleverser** to startle, shatter
**bricoler** to potter about, do odd jobs
**briller** to shine; to

sparkle
**briser** to break, smash
**brûler** to burn
**(se) cacher** to hide
**(se) calmer** to calm down
**casser** to break
**causer** to cause; to chat
**cesser (de)** to stop
**changer d'avis** to change one's mind
**chanter** to sing
**charger (de)** to load (with)
**chasser** to chase (off); to get rid of
**chauffer** to warm up, heat up
**chercher** to look for; see **aller**
**choisir** to choose
**chuchoter** to whisper
**circuler** to move (of vehicles)
**cirer** to polish
**collaborer** to collaborate
**coller** to stick
**commander** to order
**commencer (à)** to begin (to)
**compenser** to compensate for, make up for
**comporter** to comprise
**comprendre** to understand
**compter** to count; to intend to
**concerner** to concern
**conclure** to conclude
**conduire** to drive
**condamner** to condemn;

to sentence
**se conduire** to behave
**confectionner** to make
**confesser** to confess
**confirmer** to confirm
**connaître** to know (person, place)
**consacrer** to devote (time)
**conseiller** to advise
**conserver** to keep
**(se) considérer** to consider (oneself)
**consister** to consist
**consommer** to consume
**constater** to establish; to state
**constituer** to constitute, make up
**construire: faire construire une maison** to have a house built
**consulter** to consult
**contempler** to contemplate
**contenir** to contain
**continuer** to continue
**convenir** to be suitable
**copier** to copy
**se coucher** to go to bed; to lie down
**coudre** to sew
**couler** to flow
**couper** to cut (off)
**courir** to run
**couvrir** to cover
**craindre** to be afraid of, to fear
**créer** to create
**crever** to have a puncture

**crier** to shout, cry
**croire** to think; to believe
**cueillir** to pick; to capture
**cultiver** to grow, cultivate
**danser** to dance
**se débrouiller** to manage
**décharger** to unload
**déchirer** to tear
**décider (de)** to decide (to)
**se décider (à)** to make up one's mind (to)
**déclarer** to declare
**se décourager** to become discouraged
**découvrir** to discover
**décrire** to describe
**défendre** to forbid; to defend
**dégager** to clear; to extricate
**se déguiser** to disguise oneself
**demander quelque chose à quelqu'un** to ask somebody for something
**demander à quelqu'un de faire quelque chose** to ask somebody to do something
**se demander** to wonder
**demeurer** to live
**démolir** to demolish
**dénombrer** to enumerate, count
**se dépêcher** to hurry
**dépendre de** to depend on

**déplaire: cela me déplaît** I don't like it

**déposer** to put down

**déranger** to disturb

**descendre** to come or go down; to get off (train etc); to take down

**désirer** to desire, want

**dessiner** to draw

**détester** to detest

**détourner** to divert

**détruire** to destroy

**développer** to develop

**devenir** to become

**devoir** to have to (must)

**différer (de)** to differ (from), be different (from)

**diminuer** to diminish, reduce

**dire** to say, to tell

**à vrai dire** as a matter of fact

**diriger** to direct

**se diriger vers** to go towards

**discuter** to discuss

**disparaître** to disappear

**se disputer** to argue, have an argument

**dissiper** to dispel

**distinguer** to distinguish

**distribuer** to distribute

**diviser** to divide

**dominer** to overcome; to dominate

**donner** to give

**donner sur** to overlook

**dormir** to sleep

**doter (de)** to endow

(with)

**se doucher** to have a shower

**dresser** to set up

**dresser une tente** to pitch a tent

**se dresser** to stand (up)

**durer** to last

**échanger** to exchange

**s'échapper (de)** to escape (from)

**éclairer** to light (up)

**éclater de rire** to burst out laughing

**économiser** to save

**écouter** to listen (to)

**écraser** to crush

**s'écraser** to crash

**s'écrier** to exclaim, cry out

**écrire** to write

**effectuer** to carry out

**effrayer** to frighten

**s'élancer** to rush, dash

**élever** to erect; to raise

**s'élever** to rise

**emmener** to take

**empêcher (de)** to prevent (from)

**employer** to use; to employ

**emporter** to take; to carry

**emprunter quelque chose à quelqu'un** to borrow something from somebody

**encourager quelqu'un à faire** to encourage somebody to do

**s'endormir** to fall asleep
**enfermer** to imprison
**s'enfuir** to flee
**enlever** to take away; to get rid of; to take off
**s'ennuyer** to be or get bored
**enregistrer** to record
**ensevelir** to bury
**entasser** to stack
**entendre** to hear
**qu'entendez-vous par . . . ?** what do you understand by . . . ?
**entendre parler de** to hear about
**s'entendre** to agree, get on
**entourer (de)** to surround (with or by)
**entrer (dans)** to enter, go or come in(to)
**envahir** to invade
**envelopper** to wrap (up)
**envoyer** to send
**éprouver** to experience, feel
**espérer** to hope
**essayer (de faire quelque chose)** to try (to do something)
**essuyer** to wipe
**établir** to establish, set up
**étaler** to spread out
**éteindre** to put out, extinguish; to switch off
**(s')étendre** to extend; to stretch out
**étonner** to astonish

**s'étonner** to be astonished
**étouffer** to suffocate; to be stifled
**être** to be
**être assis(e)** to be sitting
**être obligé de** to be obliged to
**être de retour** to be back
**être sur le point de** to be on the point of, just about to
**être en train de faire quelque chose** to be (busy) doing something
**(s')éveiller** to wake up
**éviter (de faire)** to avoid (doing)
**examiner** to examine
**s'excuser (de)** to apologize (for)
**exister** to exist
**expliquer** to explain
**exprimer** to express
**fabriquer** to manufacture, make
**se fâcher** to become angry
**faillir: il a failli tomber** he almost fell
**faire** to do; to make
**faire attention** to be careful
**faire la connaissance de** to meet
**faire entrer quelqu'un** to let somebody in
**se faire couper les cheveux** to have one's hair cut

faire du mal (à) to harm
faire de même to do the same
faire partie de to belong to (*club etc*)
faire de son mieux (pour) to do one's best (to)
faire une promenade to go for a walk
faire remarquer to mention, point out
se faire remarquer to be noticed
faire semblant de to pretend to
faire sensation to cause a sensation
faire signe to signal, wave
il faut one must *etc*
falloir to be necessary
féliciter to congratulate
(se) fermer to close, shut
fermer à clef to lock
figurer to imagine
finir to finish
fixer to stare at; to fix
flâner to stroll, lounge about
fonctionner to work
faire fonctionner to operate
former to form
fouiller to search
fournir to provide
frapper to hit, strike, knock
fréquenter to frequent
gagner to win; to earn

garantir to guarantee
garder to keep
gâter to spoil
se gâter to go wrong
gémir to groan
gêner to bother
glisser to slip, slide
gratter to scratch
grimper to climb
guetter to watch
habiter to live (in)
hésiter to hesitate
heurter to bump into
ignorer not to know
imaginer to imagine
imprimer to print
indiquer quelque chose à quelqu'un to inform somebody of something
s'inquiéter to worry
ne vous inquiétez pas! don't worry!
inscrire to inscribe
s'inscrire to register
installer to fix (up)
s'installer to settle, sit (down)
s'instruire to educate oneself
interdire to prohibit
'interdit de fumer' 'no smoking'
intéresser to interest
s'intéresser à quelque chose to be interested in something
interroger to question
interrompre to interrupt
interviewer to interview
introduire to introduce

**inviter** to invite
**jeter** to throw (away)
**joindre** to join
**jurer** to swear
**laisser** to leave; to let; to allow
**laisser tomber** to drop
**lancer** to throw
**(se) laver** to wash
**lever** to lift; to raise
**se lever** to get up; to stand up
**lire** to read
**loger (chez)** to lodge (with), live (with)
**louer** to hire, rent
**lutter** to struggle
**manœuvrer** to operate
**manquer** to miss; to be lacking
**marcher** to walk; to work (*of object*)
**se marier (avec quelqu'un)** to marry (somebody)
**mêler** to mix
**se mêler (à quelque chose)** to be involved (in something)
**menacer** to threaten
**mener** to lead
**mentir** to lie, tell a lie
**mériter** to deserve
**tu l'as mérité!** you deserved it!
**mesurer** to measure
**mettre** to put (on); to take (*time*)
**mettre quelque chose au point** to bring something

about; to get something ready
**mettre quelqu'un à la porte** to throw somebody out
**mettre quelque chose à la poste** to post something
**se mettre à l'abri** to take shelter
**se mettre en colère** to get angry
**monter** to come *or* go up; to get into (*car etc*); to take up
**montrer** to show; to point out
**se moquer de** to make fun of
**multiplier** to multiply
**noter** to note
**nourrir** to nourish; to cherish
**obliger quelqu'un à faire** to force *or* oblige somebody to do
**observer** to observe; to keep
**obtenir** to obtain
**s'occuper de** to attend to; to be concerned with
**offrir** to give, offer
**s'opposer à** to be opposed to
**ordonner** to order, command
**organiser** to organize
**orner (de)** to decorate (with)
**oser (faire quelque**

chose) to dare (to do something)

oublier to forget

(s')ouvrir to open; to switch on

paraître to appear

parier (sur) to bet (on)

parler to speak, talk

partager to share

partir to leave, depart, go away

passer to pass; to spend (time)

passer un disque to play a record

passer un examen to sit an exam

se passer to happen

passionner to excite

pavoiser to decorate with flags

payer to pay

peindre to paint

pénétrer (dans) to enter, make one's way into

penser (à) to think (about)

penser de to have an opinion of

perdre to lose

perdre quelqu'un de vue to lose sight of somebody

permettre (à quelqu'un de faire) to allow or permit (somebody to do)

persuader to persuade

peser to weigh

photographier to photograph

placer to place, put

se plaindre (de) to complain (about)

plaire (à) to please

cela me plaît I like that

plaisanter to joke

pleurer to cry

plier to fold

porter to carry; to wear; to take

poser to put (down)

poser des questions to ask questions

posséder to possess

poursuivre to pursue

pousser to push; to grow

pousser un cri to utter a cry

pouvoir to be able to (can)

pratiquer to go in for

précipiter to hurl

se précipiter dans to rush into

prédire to predict

préférer to prefer

prendre to take

prendre feu to catch fire

prendre part à to take part in

prendre quelque chose à quelqu'un to take something from somebody

prendre soin (de) to take care (to)

préparer to prepare

présenter to present; to introduce

se présenter to appear; to introduce oneself

prêter quelque chose à

**quelqu'un** to lend somebody something

**prévoir** to foresee

**prier** to request

**je vous en prie** please, don't mention it

**priver quelqu'un de quelque chose** to deprive somebody of something

**produire** to produce

**profiter (de)** to take advantage (of)

**se promener** to go for a walk

**promettre (à quelqu'un de faire quelque chose)** to promise (somebody to do something)

**prononcer** to pronounce

**prononcer un discours** to make a speech

**proposer (de faire)** to suggest (doing)

**protéger** to protect

**provoquer** to cause

**se quereller** to quarrel

**quitter** to leave

**raconter** to tell

**ramasser** to pick up

**ramener** to bring or take back

**ranger** to arrange, tidy

**se rappeler** to remember

**rapporter** to report; to bring back

**rater** to miss; to fail

**rattraper quelqu'un** to catch up with somebody

**recevoir** to receive

**réchauffer** to warm (up)

**recommencer** to begin again

**reconnaître** to recognize

**recouvrir (de)** to cover (with)

**redescendre** to come or go down again

**refaire** to re-do, do again

**refermer** to close again

**réfléchir** to think, reflect

**refuser (de)** to refuse (to)

**regagner** to go back to

**regarder** to look (at)

**régler** to adjust; to direct (*traffic*); to settle (*bill*)

**regretter (que)** to be sorry (that)

**rejoindre** to meet; to rejoin; to reach

**se relever** to get up again

**relier** to connect

**relire** to read again

**remarquer** to notice

**rembourser** to refund

**remercier (de)** to thank (for)

**remettre** to put back; to take back; to postpone

**remonter dans** to get back into

**remplacer** to replace

**remplir (de)** to fill (with)

**remuer** to stir

**rencontrer** to meet

**rendre** to give back

**rendre visite à** to visit

**se rendre** to surrender, give oneself up

**se rendre à** to visit (*place*)

se rendre compte to realize
(se) renfermer to shut (oneself) in
renseigner to inform
se renseigner (sur) to inquire (about)
rentrer to return
renverser to overturn, knock over
renvoyer to send back
repasser to press, iron
répéter to repeat
répondre to reply
se reporter à to refer to
se reposer to rest
reprendre to resume
représenter to represent
résoudre to solve
ressembler à to resemble
ressortir to bring or take out
rester to stay, remain
retenir to book, reserve
retentir to sound
retourner to return
se retourner to turn round
retrouver to meet; to find (again)
se réunir to meet
réussir (à faire) to succeed (in doing)
se réveiller to waken up
révéler to reveal
revenir to come back
rêver to dream
rigoler, rire to laugh
risquer (de) to risk
rougir to blush

rouler to drive (along)
saisir to seize, grasp
salir to dirty
saluer to greet
sauter to jump
sauver to save
se sauver to run off
savoir to know
sécher to dry
secouer to shake
sélectionner to select
sembler to seem
sentir to smell
se sentir (mal) to feel (ill)
séparer to separate
se serrer la main to shake hands
(se) servir to serve (oneself)
se servir de quelque chose to use something
signaler to point out
signer to sign
sonner to ring
sortir to go or come out; to take out
se soucier de to worry about
souhaiter to wish
soulager to relieve
soulever to lift
soupçonner to suspect
soupirer to sigh
sourire to smile
soutenir la comparaison avec to bear comparison with
se souvenir de quelque

**chose** to remember something
**sucer** to suck
**suffire** to be sufficient
**suggérer** to suggest
**suivre** to follow
**surprendre** to surprise
**sursauter** to give a jump
**se taire** to be quiet
**tâter** to taste; to sample
**téléphoner (à)** to telephone
**tendre** to hold out
**tenter de** to attempt to
**(se) terminer** to finish
**tirer** to let off (*fireworks*); to shoot
**tomber** to fall
**laisser tomber** to drop
**tomber en panne** to break down
**toucher (à) quelque chose** to touch something
**toucher de l'argent** to receive money
**tourner** to turn
**tourner un film** to shoot a film
**se tourner vers** to turn towards
**trahir** to betray

**traîner** to drag, pull
**travailler** to work
**traverser** to cross; to go through; to go over
**tromper** to outwit
**se tromper** to be mistaken
**troubler** to worry
**trouver** to find
**se trouver** to be (situated)
**tuer** to kill
**unir** to unite
**utiliser** to use
**vaincre** to conquer
**valoir** to be worth
**vendre** to sell
**venir** to come
**venir de faire quelque chose** to have just done something
**vérifier** to check
**verser** to pour
**visiter** to visit
**vivre** to live
**voir** to see
**voler** to steal; to fly
**vouloir** to want
**vouloir dire** to mean
**voyager** to travel

The following French words have more than one translation, depending on context. If you do not already know these translations, check them up on the following pages, and then why not look for more?

Still more homonyms! Are you sure you know *all* their meanings?

## INDEXE

INDEXE

The vocabulary lists on the following pages cover the majority of nouns in the first two levels of the book, and will be a useful translation guide when you have a mental blank. A semi-colon between page numbers shows there will be a different translation depending on the context — simply look up the pages mentioned and the translation you require will be clear.